P9-CQH-424

DOING MORE
WITH ONE LIFE

A Writer's Journey through the
Past, Present, and Future

BRUCE PIASECKI

Prospecta Press

I dedicate this book to my formidable family

and fabulous wife and daughter;

may you all forgive me for writing so many books,

some about you.

Foreword

A RUMINATION ON WHAT WE FOUND IN THE WORKS OF BRUCE PIASECKI

JAY PARINI

This memoir is an eye-opener both for its frankness and for how it fits yet distorts literary traditions.

I have endorsed Bruce Piasecki's prior books, such as *Doing More with Less*, and its sequel *Doing More with Teams*. They are works of nonfiction with plenty of narrative skill in their rendering. But *Doing More with One Life* explores new territories by diving straight into the realms of poetry, psychology, self-invention, prosperity, personal narrative, and the fate of families. This is the stuff of autobiography writ large, as I learned from editing the *Norton Anthology of American Autobiography*.

Throughout, Piasecki takes us on an unexpected journey into a new form of autobiography, a life story projected and reflected. For this most dramatic book proves itself to have deep roots in American and in the Latin American traditions of magical realism. Furthermore, the author overall creates an atmosphere of pragmatic self-awareness.

This comes directly from the realms of modern business, but also indirectly from the wit and ambitions of Ben Franklin. It is this eclectic mix that proves electrifying.

Before you dive in, perhaps you'd find this useful to frame your expectations. For any judicious review of literature will suggest that autobiography lies at the dead center of the American enterprise—not a surprising fact, given that American history presupposes a radical sense of equality, one in which the individual is celebrated.

Walt Whitman's "Song of Myself" is truly our national anthem, although the self that Whitman celebrates moves well beyond petty individualism: this is the song of the American self, the common man who becomes, through awareness, education, and hard work, a distinct part of a larger whole.

As a distinct genre, autobiography was pioneered by Ben Franklin, the father of the form in its American incarnation, which is always the story of how a boy from nowhere cobbled together a life, found his footing in the world, and transformed that world along with himself, making himself part and parcel of a peculiar universe, one of his own self-invention. The genre migrates through various narrative modes, such as the journey of Henry

David Thoreau to the edge of the village, where he builds a house of self on the shores of Walden Pond and discovers the universe. It reaches through the immigrant narratives of figures such as Mary Antin, who, in *The Promised Land,* put forward a paradigm of assimilation that has inspired generations of arrivals to these shores. It snakes through the narratives of Frederick Douglass and W. E. B. Du Bois, who framed the debate over race in America for all time, and moves through such great contemporary classics as Hemingway's *A Moveable Feast* or Annie Dillard's gorgeous *Pilgrim at Tinker Creek.* The genre seems endlessly protean, open to fresh voices and forms, expansive.

Bruce Piasecki has added his own twist to the endlessly repeatable tale of self-invention, tracking a spiritual journey through love and faith, family and friends. *Doing More with One Life* is a book about the absences that define our lives, the tears in the fabric that we spend a lifetime trying to repair. It's about what the poet Elizabeth Bishop called "The art of losing," and yet each loss foretells a gain, as Piasecki reshapes his life, rediscovers lost family and friends, and connects to literary ancestors—some of whom, like Walt Whitman, lend a layer of texture and allusion to his prose that makes it not only readable but re-readable.

As an ex-basketball player, Piasecki does not presume he can jump as high as Ben Franklin or Whitman or Jonathan Edwards or Casanova, just a few of the writers he channels. Instead, in an unpretentious, tactical, and sure-footed way, he examines the events that shaped his own life through the lens of these great writers, inhabiting what he calls the "neighborhood" of their lives.

Their books are his neighbors and friends throughout this memoir, and he echoes them at every turn.

Piasecki's inventive memoir includes over seventy interrelated vignettes—tiny nuggets of narration that nest within the larger narrative arc as the author describes his growing self-awareness, a slowly widening sense of the world. The vignettes move in a roughly chronological fashion, but some of them play back and repeat certain themes and motifs—as with key characterizations of the author's long-dead father, Walter, his generous mother Lillian, his lovely daughter Colette, and his strong wife Varlissima. These characters dance in his head, and their voices underpin his own. They appear and disappear, flash and fade.

Piasecki is a natural postmodernist, and he plays easily—one might almost say fast and loose—with time, as in the final section, where he writes the autobiography of his future. He builds on understandings already attained, while shaping a larger understanding of his own selfhood in response to the world. Indeed, this is a work of fiction in the truest sense. That is, it's about creating narratives by highlighting some themes, hiding others. As the author dances around the absences in his life, he uses language itself—a supple instrument in his hands—to create new wholes, to fill spaces, to make a life of ampleness and plenitude.

This is a fresh and highly readable contribution to the art of autobiography. It has narrative thrills and the *frissons* of poetic insights. By accretion and artful juxtaposition, the author builds a life. But once contemplated in full, and in relationship to his other books and accomplishments, a bigger pattern emerges. This is not just a reflection on the life of Bruce Piasecki, businessman and scholar, entrepreneur and family man. Piasecki becomes, in effect, every man here, dramatizing the sorrows and joys that come into our lives, taking us through his experiences, allowing us to enter his world in ways that become our world, as readers. That is a gift that keeps yielding, part Whitmanesque, part Shakespearean, and always Piasecki.

Jay Parini is a noted writer and Professor of English at Middlebury College in Vermont. He is the author of distinguished books of poetry; biographies of Robert Frost, John Steinbeck, and Jesus Christ; as well as a number of novels. He also edited the Norton Anthology of American Autobiography. Jay's historical novel The Last Station, *was made into an Academy Award-nominated film starring Helen Mirren.*

Preface
CRACKING THE CODE

Sigmund Freud, a masterful writer, and fanciful thinker, begins his *Interpretation of Dreams* in a curious and compelling fashion. I read it while an undergraduate at Cornell. I have never forgotten the opening passages.

Freud starts his personal narrative by having the reader feel a fearful dream about his father. While the book is scholarly, and detailed, and full of speculation and intellectual surprise, the text itself has lasted many decades because it consists of a personal narrative. It is the pace of the prose, and the dignity in the narrative's fears and joys, that enable us to imagine the feelings of dread and responsibility about the death of anyone's father.

Freud, like Darwin and Karl Marx, is a fantastic storyteller.

I will not quote the Freud passage. It is an articulate twenty pages. Instead, I will convey now the passage's overall creative force—as it hit me some forty-four years ago, while I was discerning if I should be a pre-med student, a business leader, or pursue more volcanic and impossible literary ambitions.

You will find in these subsequent pages that I've sat beside each of these interests for a long life now, unable to stop a fire burning inside of me, yet unable in my daily fixations to choose one life over another. Businessman, a reader in science, medicine, and literature—or a writer's life. Books, many of them, were the bridges that enabled these sustaining and useful interests.

LIVING THE CODE

I can still see Freud with his father, in his grand European Jewish funeral service, dressed in proper attire. This passage proved so consuming for me because, when I was three years old, on a bathroom floor near my parents' bedroom, I tried to wake my father. He was dying of a cerebral hemorrhage, spitting blood. I failed.

In Freud's passage, his family has already shared their grief for the appropriate number of prayers and hours; but the young doctor Freud in his dream stays after. A part of any memoir is rumination, the staying after the hour of panic has passed, lingering after the minute of joy has expired.

Tired from his medical work, and emotionally drained by the death of his father, the doctor in this dream falls asleep near his father. Exhausted, yet in a vivid dream, two candles drop into his father's coffin, igniting the body. Perhaps (I do not recall) there were similar tears that fell to my father's face.

The fire consumes the elder's clothes, then the coffin itself, and then the father, in a dream that becomes Freud's insight into Oedipal impulses. I learned very little in facing my father's death except that writing gave me a chance to defy an early death. While you may question the universality of Freud's fear—our ordinary lives of business competition make Freud's musings seem like a distracting fancy, even an indulgence—yet the desire to kill your predecessors and competitors to find your own voice is felt and repeated in many families. I read of the same set of impulses each week in *Worth* magazine, the *Financial Times* of London, in the popular press. We are a competitive species, for sure. Some of these vignettes portray and explore these basic impulses.

A personal obligation to lifelong writing comes with obliterating forces. I saw this most days in my nine years of training at Cornell University, in what should have been a placid place near Lake Cayuga. Great and good writers strive to erase or to surpass their mentors, what Harold Bloom of Yale called "The Anxiety of Influence."

I knew I could not surpass my dissertation teacher, M. H. Abrams, or his friend the great poet Archie Ammons, my wife's advisor. But I felt the need to try. The arrogance of youth is explored in the first third of this collection.

WHY THIS BOOK

This collection of vignettes provides glimpses at the creative force that remains propulsive in my life, this angst, this oscillation from the fears and joys that consume a writer's life. Part two explores the maturing of these emotions and experiences in both business and in this writer's life.

Each vignette is a miniature meant to help the reader crack a code as ancient as Sumerian cuneiform. You expect to be informed, persuaded, and delighted. You will turn away and you will leave me without that force.

I do this knowing the weight of all before you. You have bills to pay, places to go, games to watch. You may not feel the same need for distinction, but I doubt it. Everyman's struggles with an imagined father, all writers, male and female, rich and poor, struggle to differentiate their voice, or dive into the average and the accepted.

By the mid-sections of this book, you find me flinging a series of biographies and fables, and materials into the waves, to see what will float or sink. Why did I do this, across more than twenty books in forty-plus editions?

A writer is made, not born. While Jack London aptly claims that a sailor is born, not made, I feel the opposite in a creative life. A man who will take to the sea in a fabric composed of wood and iron and lots of ropes is different from a writer striking out at the internal and external seas of their imagination. Writing requires an odd and persistent will that does not obey simple surfaces or even the terrible turbulence discernible to sailors at sea. Herein you will find the storyline of a journey that could not have been predicted, considering my origins.

For me, writing has always involved a kind of protest song. My life has been a tale organized in stanzas against the magic box of diminished expectations where we are first born to babble, a place in my case of anticipated factory service near the railroad tracks, a place where my athletic coaches wanted me to serve them milk on the basketball court like a Devon cow. It is all so different now. The final third in this collection explains what's valuable about the arc in a life.

I provide this without anger but with feeling, and vivid memories of the striving to escape or to excel my original selves. The middle parts of this book recreate, in detail, those feelings of striving and ascending. The finale offers resolutions and success.

WHEN ONE ENDS

No book remains for long. Every book is a crumbling brick of hacked shapes and meanings—I see each of my prior books now as I see my favored petroglyphs beside their ancient Southwest Indian ruins.

Each book was a try, an attempt, an effort to share with you. By the last portion of my career, I am surrounded by being three things at once, family man, business owner, and writer. With a pile of books beside me.

Yet all this came with panic and resolve, with artful joy and propulsive fears. As I approach the end, I am aware of a million stars brighter than our best dreams. Expect this feeling in the concluding vignettes: I found in art and in prose a sustaining hope, where daily composition sustained a learned defiance of simple despair.

Today, I stand on the shoulders of Sigmund Freud, Charles Darwin, Karl Marx, and a mountain of others who stand on even larger and more ancient shoulders, parties with friends long past. Much in the world's first writing I can now feel in me, and in reading and meeting others, carved in clay tablets, hard to discern, but clearly human transactions at the dawn of human history, more than 5000 years old. Somehow, I learned to convert a physical body into what Ammons calls a word body, a corpus.

Some of the feelings in these vignettes are ancient feelings, as old as the Sumerians. To me, an avid conversationalist, all humans seem to need to record a mark, a strike against the darkness that surrounds. Perhaps this explains why "memoir" has become a most popular form of books, movies, and storytelling today across the globe. I love my talks on trains, in supermarkets, in bookstores, in the malls.

In these pages meet the magical clan of writers who helped me become myself. They helped me strike out against the rocks that faced me, my firm, and my family. Feel in these pages a primordial need. I find that my need to write was there from before high school— perhaps when I stood confused above my father's early death—and this need proved a muscle that I exercised most weeks, and most days.

This book is a collection of those things I told myself in notebooks, now reshaped for your use. Perhaps these offer a few pebbles you can use in your constructs.

—Saratoga Springs, March 2023

Part One

THE DISCOVERY OF COLETTE

(VIGNETTES OF INNOCENCE AND YOUTH)

"We have our secrets, and our needs to confess.
We may remember, in childhood,
adults were able to look right through us,
and into us, and what an accomplishment
it was when we, in fear and trembling,
could tell our first lie."

—R. D. Laing, *The Divided Self*

UNCLE ZIGMUND, LONG ISLAND

Uncle Ziggy walked in strength, carrying his Polish heritage in his stride. He would not take bad news or misbehavior from anyone. Even many years later, he could hear the click in that walk, Uncle Ziggy's swagger. Uncle Zigmund brought the Old World out of him, and the New World into him.

Standing strong and bronzed from his work as a Long Island landscaper, Uncle Ziggy had the build of a Polish Hercules. Zigmund was a funny man, a sportive man, a big friendly man. People smiled when near him. That was his gift to the New World.

"The people out there," he would say in his half-earnest, half-jovial Polish accent, "they give me a typed list of things to do—some sod here, some pines there, some new pruning here. They do not know what they really want! So I bury the list and do what *I* want. And they thank me. America is wonderful."

Members of Ziggy's extended family—from curious cousins to outraged adults—adopted this New World technique of defiantly ignoring the landowners. They too, would rip up their lists, and proceed boldly. He found this his first hint on how to handle the revisions and independence found in a writer's life.

"I had a toothache," Zigmund once said at Christmas dinner. "So I drank half a bottle of vodka—good vodka, the best—but the pain was still there. I got in my new car. I was on the Long Island Expressway before I knew it. Something in me said I'd better get off this wide highway, not to miss the turn to the dentist. I did as my mind told me to do. I swayed off the road a little, and took a nap near the turn. When I woke up, the tooth hurt even more, so I drank the other half of the bottle. When I got to the dentist's office—where I noticed that he could use some more of my shrubs—the receptionist asked me, 'Do you have an appointment?'"

Knitting together his thick eyebrows, Zigmund paused for the punch line. "Hey, you folks are a joke. You give me an appointment when I know no pain, and now that I am full of pain you cannot help me. I thought America was the land of opportunity. Where is the opportunity, Doc, to fix this damn tooth?"

Ziggy had a son who made it to Notre Dame on a football scholarship. Zigmund would call him collect in South Bend, Indiana: "Hello operator, good day to you Madame, this is Zigmund Yashevski calling Zigmund Yashevski. Please connect me now." Again and again, there would be a click at the other end—as the Lily

Tomlin-like operator, imagining Uncle Ziggy to be no more than a prankster, hung up. Bruce thought about the oddness in Ziggy's insistence every time he found himself making that extra phone call for business. Zigmund was always there, egging him on to make that extra call even when they hung up.

Loud and colorful alarms went off in his young head, whenever he spent any time with Uncle Zigmund —the outspoken but victorious rebel of the family, the guy who thought he could make something of his life in this new America.

INTERRACIAL FOSTER BROTHERS AND SISTERS

Edwin Torres and Suie Ying Chang were his brother and sister, his Adam and Eve. While he had watched other foster brothers and sisters, from different races, from distant regions, come and go, Edwin and Suie stayed the longest in his memories.

While he had other people press near him now that he was a high school basketball star, it was the bounce and hope in Edwin's voice and Suie' s dark round eyes that tracked his moods the most in his youth. When they were sad, so was he. He felt that he was their protector, and the only one in his neighborhood thinking about where their next dollar might come from. He felt these foster brothers and sisters depended on him. He knew this in a primal way, in a way that was deeper than the prejudices that surrounded him.

After his father, Walter, died, the Veteran's and social security benefits were not adequate to feed and clothe the family. He saw that early in life. While his teachers and coaches chose to ignore such topics, he knew he would need to earn his way out of this predicament.

His mother could not afford a car. They never ate out. The only book of consequence in the house was the Bible. He started working at age ten—washing white walls on cars, working as a landscaper on Mongoon's Landing, laying sod like his Uncle Ziggy—to build that family purse. Lillian, his mom, left factory work and opened their home to foster children, which gave them a small but steady income. Locked into this arrangement, he felt close to his foster brothers and sisters most of the time. He remembers that fine day when he first received his working papers at the Rotunda of Beach Street. He was in his teens, and he felt at last ready to serve them.

Edwin was Puerto Rican and hyperkinetic—always rocking, always moving, always in trouble at school. "Edwin is a monster," a principal told him at Westbrook, many years before he had learned to fight back with words. They said Edwin was hyperkinetic because his biological parents were heroin addicts. Edwin was the only brother that stayed for more than six years, until he went missing. Most of the others were adopted by other families in a matter of months or a few years. He viewed this as a message. The accumulated worth of those losses defined his sense of what was missing in his life.

Suie Ying was born with birthmarks on her arms and legs, purplish maps that told the nuns at the New

York City Catholic Foundling Home that she was a mix
of Han Chinese and Samoan. Margaret Mead herself
had once looked over her smallish body. Dr. Mead pro-
nounced Suie Ying "special and odd." There were other
scars on Suie Ying's young body from a mother who had
left her on a lit stove in Spanish Harlem. But that was
before she found her real mother in Lillian.

His biological sister, Terry, was five years older than
he, a saint-like Teresa, named after her patron saint.
Never wronging any of the new foster kids, always
praying for them, striving to be good before the peering
eyes of God. Terry would marry her first high school
sweetheart, Richard, and raise a smart lawyer daughter
Samantha. His Long Island cousins were ever-present,
warm, and caring family members, and neighbors during
the reign of Suie and Edwin. Chris died in his late forties;
Diane moved south. Steven grew proud and distant.

In contrast to his biological and foster siblings, he was
an angry young man. By age fifteen, he had turned his
athletic training into a weapon. This made him firmly
capable of harming people on and off the court. He was
a three-letter man during high school: a point guard
on the basketball court, an aggressive center half on the
soccer field, a shot putter and captain of the track team.
All of these sports left scars—"knees of a hundred-year-
old," his first surgeon noted; but he knew he had caused
more harm to others than to himself. He called the scars
"battle wounds," and wore them with some pride.

At home at 358 Oakwood Avenue, his mother Lillian
and his wonderfully generous Aunt Ann cooked for at
least a dozen of them on weekends. His Uncle Steve was
never far off—always ready to give him a lift to a job.

Uncle Steve's eyes were so bad they saved him from the draft, so he was always there—steady, kind, and loving.

Uncle Steve, a janitor at the local junior high, had a light-green van big enough to take the extended family all over Long Island—and to Mass at Our Lady of Lourdes Church in West Islip. Bruce came to love most of the Island that this van could reach, and he blissfully ignored the rest. Dix Hills and Northport and Oyster Bay were other worlds, the realm of royalty, and as far off from his imagination and longing as the moon before JFK.

The van lasted a good decade, from when he was age seven to seventeen.

Somehow this crowded, active absence allowed him to develop a feverish and a sportive view of his life. He learned to take heed of small immediate pleasures like a mother's meal—the crisp crusts of her apple pies—but he still knew what his distant, invisible father meant when he said that life was "one damned thing after another."

He ran everywhere, dribbling his basketball. Years later, he would find that Lillian had saved this worn basketball in her attic. Beneath the ceaseless bounce in the game, the resentments of poverty sat still and angry. He was freed during game times.

THE EMPTY HOUSE,
LONG ISLAND

The empty house, abandoned but near, proved a perfect unexpected spot for teenage passion. Mary Beth had discovered the house across Montauk Highway, not far from her St. John's Catholic High School. He could still hear the cars rush by, racing for an advantaged position up the ramp to Robert Moses Bridge and his favorite white sand beach.

Mary Beth's father made films in Manhattan. Her mother—interested in his early poetry—was on the West Islip Library Board. Like her mom, Mary Beth never used their massive home to lord over him. Her father played cards with author Mario Puzo in the dining room, she said, before Puzo became famous for writing *The Godfather* as well as the screenplay for the award-winning movie of the same name.

The afternoon that Mary Beth brought him to the abandoned house, he was in faded shorts and a T-shirt marked from landscaping. Mary Beth said she liked the smell of grass and turf, boy and man. And it was Mary Beth, so tiny, who encouraged this early trespass.

It felt fine to him as well, being able to be in town, yet so far from the sight of his world near the tracks. But he also felt it far too easy, far too natural. While his shorts slipped down, he realized in a long repetitive playback, it was not his, but rather Mary Beth's trespass. He would come to see that later. Back then, however, he fancied it his conquest.

The abandoned couch was in better shape than the one he occasionally slept on at home. Whenever his knee hurt too much to climb up the ladder (built by Walter) to his own bunk bed, which he shared with siblings, he would sleep on the couch in the living room.

That day, Mary Beth caressed the back of his right knee. She was intuitive, athletic, easing exactly the spot where the pain centered, where the tear slowed his basket-ball game. He was now ready to return to practice with Coach Smith. She wanted him to stay with her. Mary Beth stood there in a strange light, demanding that he stay.

He picked up her colorful steel bangles from the purple sofa and placed them back on her thin but not fragile wrists. Mary Beth had the wrists of a tennis player and the thighs of a runner. Despite the strength of her request, despite the power in her stance, he noticed how her demands had no sway over him.

He moved on. The abandoned home remained for several decades before it fell. St. John's Catholic School, its icons still intact, continues to function by genuflection and need.

AN ANGRY
YOUNG MAN

His four years of varsity basketball meant everything to him. More than even his select books. His team played against powerful opponents like Brentwood. A *Newsday* journalist wrote of him as "Chicken Little," saying he could bring down the sky with his long shot. He failed to be completely joyful in his victories, as he knew others were watching to prevent his further play. That fear made him both ready and angry.

Decades later, he could still recall most of the games he'd been in—major league or pickup—and most of the moves he had gotten away with. The bank shots that had swirled around and around and then dropped in meant everything to him. Anger may have urged a shot, but it was good fortune that allowed the swoosh. He was a shooter—and a performer—from day one on the courts.

Coach Smith spotted this ability to thrill, to absorb the limelight, early in him, in eighth grade—moving him up to varsity at age fourteen for four years in the spotlight. On the court, he turned his rage into winning baskets by driving the baseline, taking hits from the bigger players, and converting the third point in a free throw. He would not smile, they said, but just do it again. If an opponent figured that move would be likely again, he'd pull up rapidly with a soft sweet classic jumper.

In memory, he was mostly that angry young man.

The game of basketball transformed his focus. The stoic rage of his youth became acceptable to parents and lovers and teachers because of basketball. He jokingly referred to this as his "MVP license," not having a driver's license let alone a car. And he knew, deep down, he didn't even need to hit every important shot for them to remain pleased with him. The point was to take the risk for the town, to make the move, earn with spit and fire the crowd's respect and wonder. By his last high school playing season, he was worn and hurt, but there were thousands in his stands. When he shot his free throws, he never heard a word.

For the rest of his life, he cultivated the thrill of being a serious shooter during game time. Indeed, it was his willingness to shoot, to make the try with focus and zeal, that helped him move from being the kid of a factory worker to the kid on a scholarship at Cornell University.

The early death of his father, the life of poverty before college, the sweaty fear that he would never prove to be a writer of consequence—these things could have made him a bitter and nasty man, another petty man. Transformed. Erect. More certain. These made him what he was: persistently self-inventive. Angry, and young. Angry in his belly, and self-inventive.

WITH MARCUS AURELIUS

When he was older, he read about wondrous cognitive mapping techniques that made it possible for shrinks to watch a troubled patient's thought paths. The strange thing was that he felt, as early as the 1970s, that he could do the same on his own, with his own life—without a machine and without the tools of science. The early death of his father gave him this intuitive gift—this ability to perceive himself in the third person, to see himself assume the form of a shot both before and while it occurred. He could watch himself watch himself without tape, without machines.

This third-person gaming became habitual to him. He was a third person, he felt.

The habit grew from year to year, and it allowed him to stop short of the mirroring that had brought down

Narcissus. Soon the gift became whimsical, sportive, a fun part of every day. It wasn't too serious; it was sportive seriousness. The right tone to adopt in a life with little.

During his twenties and thirties, he came to feel that he was watching thoughts, rather than actors and actresses, in all the greatest films he had ever seen. He could still remember his first Fellini film, and how it helped him realize that he had watched his entire life as if it had been a film; not in sequence, but in passion. He had learned how to "perform while withdrawn." This phrase—from one of his early poems—stuck with him.

The strange, stern, thug-like thought paths of Marcus Aurelius grooved his mind during those days off the court; Mr. Plumer, his best high school teacher, had given him his own paperback edition of the emperor's *Meditations.*

Aurelius helped him get past the good-boy looks of his yearbook. He was now a bastard on the court, and now fierce in his mind. After reading Marcus Aurelius, he would be awakened by night sweats, by a froth stirred in his dreams. During the day, he'd catch himself thinking he could control Coach Smith during time-outs, twist the crowd when on the court, shape their thoughts to understand his game.

WITH LEFTY AT THE U OF MARYLAND

He was in his prime in College Park, on summer scholarship, to see if he could play Big Ten basketball. He was only sixteen, but still the legendary coach recruited him. With Lefty as his summer coach, the world widened past his back alleys into something more surprising, and jovial.

He took his heady view of himself into summer camp with new sneakers from Wolfe's in Rockville Center. He viewed his body like a joke. He felt convinced that this gave him the sportive right to talk of himself in this third person, to play hoop his entire life.

This became a habitual form of self-reflection, even in his college applications.

"Bruce will get the graham crackers after he gets the milk for his mom, and will then apply to Yale before Princeton," the Princeton application recorded, stating this a "practical way to size up his chances." He knew a serious candidate would not mention graham crackers in a college application, and he knew enough of his chances to be spoofing Princeton by mentioning Yale first.

He viewed it all as a joke. Otherwise, the world opening before him because he could dribble a ball was far too large. Nonetheless, the authorities must have all thought him a lunatic! Even in high school, he acted the role of Marcus Aurelius in class—austere, articulate, and self-determining, on and off the court, controlling his crowds. Yet he played hoop with abandon.

This all peaked for him during a summer scholarship in 1972, a full ride with meals and clothes, to the Lefty Driesell Basketball Camp at the University of Maryland. The gym was huge, the meals were remarkable, his teammates were fundamentally faster and better than any he had ever played with. Lefty Dreisell, by now a legendary coach at UMD, gave him on the side extra cash, meals, and a bigger head for sweeping the floor when others left for rest. Perhaps his cousin Steven was right: he was becoming "Cousin Big Head." His wingspan kept growing as well; soon his shoulders resembled those of Uncle Ziggy and those of his cousin Zigmund, who played football for Notre Dame.

He said to himself each late afternoon that summer, "but Bruce could use an even bigger body," as he swept. He felt often that his head was too heavy for the rest of his body, so he kept lifting more and more weights to reshape his upper torso. His legs had already been shaped from the miles of cutting lawns, from when he was ten to the end of high school. He felt all this running was the best way for him to appreciate his born limits. He'd run ten to twenty miles a day to find better and better pick-up games, some in Babylon, some in Bay Shore, and the best in Brentwood.

He liked sweeping for the coach's cash at the University of Maryland's big-time floor. He was proud pushing that broom. Lefty's brooms were always like brand new, so much fresher than the worn and warped broom he grew up with in West Islip. Lillian's sole broom had been worn into a tilt.

In College Park, at age sixteen, he walked with the legends of the game.

Already over 225 pounds of upper arm and leg muscle, at six feet one inch, he hung out each day with Mitch Kupchak, at six feet eleven inches. Mitch was a natural center. Bruce was not a natural star—some thought of Bruce as a six-foot, 225-pound point guard who could shoot "unnatural." Point guards are supposed to be lean, swift, and severe. He was neither lean nor swift, but many found him coachable. Mitch would star in college, get hurt early as a pro, and then by the new century become General Manager of the Los Angeles Lakers. Mitch was not the only UMD camper that summer who would turn pro.

Guarding as best he could Earl "the Pearl" Monroe for a week of camp, running near Kevin Laugherty of the Baltimore Bullets—and a few times, scoring over Kevin but not Earl—those were the days of wonder. He hung with many college-bound future pros, like Kenny Henry, realizing they were destined for jail, or the street, or the biggest leagues. Kenny could dunk from a standstill, effortlessly. Some of Kenny's behavior, like wearing a dog chain around his neck, frightened Coach Lefty.

Lefty asked Bruce to "reason with Kenny if he wants to be with you on the all-star pickup game next week."

Never good at patience or skilled in impulse control, Kenny Henry removed the dog chain with his naked hands at mid court, and kept running, throwing the chain at the coach on the bench. Kenny starred that week in the all-star game. Yet like so many, he was jailed as a big black before the end of the next year, never making it to college.

Thinking about how to outsmart the plight of Kenny Henry, he now became aware of how limited his body proved that summer. He began to ask Marcus: Could any of this innate anger and competitiveness be translated into a life outside the court?

His right knee was in constant pain, his left having its first cartilage tear that season. He had never contemplated college before, so he was hyper alert in his chair. He began to answer the application requests, all coming in from friends of his high school coach.

One night he remembered to take his life seriously. His sister Terry, their grandmother, and his mother were preoccupied with their favorite TV comedy show. Suie and Edwin paused in their shenanigans.

The laughter from downstairs lingered as he thought about his near future. He would resist going downstairs with his family until he completed the mission, until he controlled the thought.

Then he got it: unlike those who consume themselves in immediacy, he could balance his lust with the thoughts of Aurelius.

He then thought long and hard about Sally, then about Mary Beth, then again about the muscular leanness in Sally's thighs, before he approached either of them in school. He often stood near them in silence, provoking them to speak first—as a stupid test of his manhood and his needs.

This ability to see himself in the third person gave him a choice to resist immediately. He could choose Sally or Mary Beth. He could succeed in this college or that one. He was playing another kind of game. This game of the personal narrative, that ceaseless game of fear and joy, in tournaments of self-invention.

He was now on scholarship at Cornell, a lowly freshman in Ithaca. He met within a few weeks a graduate student. Sandy seemed to have come from a different part of the world, an Elizabethan place of sparkle and hope, and this he found an early example of plentitude. He found it a worthy game to test his heart and his words. "Speak low," she noted, "if you speak love."

They shared the attention of M. H. Abrams, one of Cornell's most distinguished professors of literary history. She would stay after class as much to hang with the new boy in class as with Professor Abrams. That pipe-in-hand legend of literary history taught them much.

She was of Russian descent, sweet as summer could find, and he was purebred Polish. He thought of himself as Polish. They were attracted to each other. Some days, she would wiggle his big toe after the mid-afternoon Ithaca storms, and, eye to eye, they would talk of literature, line by line. He found that he could use language to draw her near—and in touching her with words, he would lighten and strengthen their mortal and magical bond for life.

One bright day in May, looking like an angel, she asked, "Do you remember that classic Polish story *Bapci's*

Angel, where the young boy's toe begins to wiggle in the hospital after his little brother prays exactly as his grandmother told him to? The motif works, doesn't it, Bruce, for both of us?" After a nod, they would melt into a sameness that only youthful sex allows.

This was 1976, and he was now twenty-one, a man in bloom. It was pure passion, with little restraint. The numbers seventy-six and twenty-one seem magical even today, when he crosses them. Back then, he still talked like a crewman. His brethren were certain his thick Long Island accent would fade away. Someday it would, like a fade away corner shot.

She was as beautiful as shooting stardust in the storybooks of old Russia. They shared a love of painted Easter eggs, and sweet Greek breakfasts downtown.

He had at about this time his first original thought: *I can have more—more of this storm, more from this soft warmth in Sandy's hands, this perpetual feeling from sex and talk after sex—and perhaps way more from literature than I was first told I could.*

Somehow, through Sandy, study had assumed increasing power. Over time, he built a worldview from his early longing for Sandy. "Hell," he thought, "if I can earn the attention of someone like Sandy, maybe it is all worth the time and trouble?" He imagined reading thousands of classics.

The gloom of his birth began to lift when he thought of her. Without knowing it, she helped him stay in Ithaca a full ten years. Even up there in icy Ithaca, he could still feel the wind from Long Island. His past, the ice, Sandy—they all mixed his memories into a frenzy of uncontrollable ambition and anger. After the many storms experienced with Sandy, he knew that life could be so much more than where he first belonged.

She was a hurricane.

She was his coach.

He was beyond being Polish. He was born again, alive in a way beyond Long Island.

THE BLIND ALLEY
OF BIRTH

Returning home one mid-term, he was amazed to realize that often his muses lingered as he moved from scene
to scene; they traveled wherever he traveled.

The blind alley of his birth was an efficient way to
describe the immediacy of the memories that haunted him.

His blind alley was the area surrounding his first
home on Oakwood Avenue. He could wander anywhere,
but he was still walking Oakwood Avenue, a blind alley
that defined him far fuller than his decade of women
at Cornell ever could. Would he ever learn to tame the
beasts within him, that seemed to grow from the traumas
of his first home?

Here was the paradox of youth in a nutshell.

He did not choose his mother. Yet his mother shaped
him.

He lent Lillian money in time, and she said, "You owe me your life!" or "Get the mop!" He realized in retrospect that it was profoundly stupid to expect any cash repayment from his mother. She was the pond, the winter, and the thaw.

She was his mother, and that was everything.

Throughout his youth he had run along this blind alley, grooved from the start—accepting the sweet gestures of Sandy as if they were distractions from the known, thrown as he was into this lovely game of life.

And then suddenly, his mother helped him look up. His mother made him restlessly look up, like a prompt frog at dawn that escapes the descent of the first storm. He leaped into the next pond, with less fear of drowning. She helped him get that freeze out of his eyes.

Under Lillian's vigilant and watchful eyes, he finished his dissertation on "Walt Whitman and the American Estimate of Nature" despite barely considering college during his high school years.

In comparison to Lillian, everything else seemed seasonal.

HIS MOTHER VISITED
HIM IN ITHACA

Evenings proved reflective. Game time over, he still had the energy and stimulus aflame. One February day, about a year after his discovery of Sandy, while now a new graduate student at Cornell, he imagined his mother aged, and near death.

He knew this to be perverse. But he also knew it to be necessary.

He was still a young man, no more than twenty-two, and she was still an active woman in her fifties, living alone on Long Island, with full control of her faculties. But during this particular visit to her son now settled in Ithaca, he chose to imagine her near death.

It was part of the perversity in his third-person view; everything must be seen from a distance. He must be prepared for anything. He had watched the early death of his father, so why not witness the loss of his mother?

It was during that visit, that stark February week, when his boots were etched with ice, that she showed him how to construct a response to this jack-in-the-box life. She knew that he was getting lost in his memories, that he was taxed by his past.

With humor and some remorse, she suggested that he face the work world. He had to learn how to father himself sooner rather than later. "Why not come back with me to factory life?" she asked.

This broke the freeze. Nothing should be taken for granted when a mother tells a tale of a return to harsh origins like that. She was telling him to see past Cornell, see past the certain professorships, into what he must become—or else return, forever.

Before success, even before aspirations, Lillian's stories showed him a sweet, ripe, pear-like middle way.

Before the declarations in Christ,

Before the conversations of Socrates,

Before the resolve of a Marcus Aurelius,

She kept him clothed. She kept him young, despite the rigid demeanor and repressions inherent in graduate training.

She called them "elaborations," these stories he would share, stark "embellishments." When home, or over the phone, she told him these stories nearly every afternoon. When faced with something complex, he would always ask himself, "Well, what choice would Lillian offer?" Her tales were more basic, more fundamental than those that tied themselves onto every word of Christ or Socrates or Aurelius. It wasn't an exact script she had offered him. It was a mother's path for him to grow past his father.

HER COAT
OF COLORS

Our purpose in life is a mystery. His primary mother, the mother he saw every day of his youth, taught him to be alert and tender in the face of this mystery. Yet there was also another astonishing Lillian; tough, persistent, driven Lillian. He called this Lillian his "second mother."

Without a father, he felt he was entitled to celebrate a "second mother." Throughout his life, he found himself expecting women to have more than themselves in themselves, maybe because of their ability to bring life into the world. In looking at the deep strengths of his mother, he came to expect women to be volcanic, with a creative doubleness that brought the mystery of a man closer to himself—like when an artist first finds his most significant muse. This mystery in women also added to his sense of their valor.

When he left his first mother Lillian at her home on Oakwood Avenue to explore Cornell, this second mother got closer to him. This second, more authoritative mother grew in him each year as he physically grew more distant from West Islip. She taught him to accept his place by not stopping, to embrace the mystery that led to his calling by roaming a larger world. She taught him an openness that knew his place but wanted more.

Like Dolly Parton, she was a woman of spirit, focus, persistence, and impact. She did not want material matters to weigh them down. Storytelling was their salvation. He was a man born to be a roamer, someone who had to test her principles against his larger world, again and again.

After a while, he concluded that this toughness, this persistence in Lillian, was something all women have within, but that these muse-like qualities are easier to access when the woman is free from a living husband. This belief in the power within single women resonated with his experiences with many basketball stars, whose moms raised the big boys themselves. Later, in business, he found this pattern often visible in the fiercest start-up enterprisers. It was not a consistent requirement for small business success, but he saw this often, this birth of the bold.

By the time he was in graduate school, he had come to believe that single mothers should be offered space in the Poets' Corner in Westminster Abbey, near the sharp nose and face mask of William Blake. But they are not even invited to the abbey. Instead, they walk home, with greasy hands from making millions of fasteners at the Dzus factory near the Long Island Railroad tracks, where he began.

So he would figure out other ways to celebrate the greatness in his second mom. Often the attempts proved futile, as if the act of her greatness was enough. There was something about this second mom that was invisible to others—something that only he could see.

He remembered his first trip back from Europe on scholarship, while he was a young Clarkson professor. He had saved his per diem to buy his mother an Austrian trail coat: bright blue, with red trim, and the traditional emblem blazing.

She never wore it.

Decades later, he was helping her move some things out of her closet, and he asked why she had never worn the coat.

She said, "I would always rather be with you as I am, than become some made-up person I am not."

VISITING THE CATHOLIC FOUNDLING HOME

Three stories capture the grace, the force, and the fascination of Lillian. Each provided lasting lessons. He remembers receiving two of those lessons as a young boy, during train rides back from Manhattan after visits to the Catholic Foundling Home. The third came decades later.

The first: "Bruce, when you meet guys like those you compete against on the basketball court or in business—just treat them with love. They will eventually do you and your family a lot of good." She taught him so much about life, and about the control of anger. She taught him the difference between hanging his life up to dry in hollow expectations, and finding the right fit for his coat, and moving on.

The second: Another time, returning from a visit to the foundling home, he and his mother encountered a large rude beast who spoke to Lillian in an ugly way about the multi-racial kids who were "taking up space" on the train. "Bruce, leave a guy like that alone, for in two or three years he will explode on his own."

He might have been ten at the time, and large enough to take a good swing at the man. Instead, she taught him how to do so much more with less, how to benefit from emotions rather than swim in them forever. They let the rude beast sit alone.

The third: One sunny June day at his home across the street from the Old Stone Church, his mother surprised him again, deeply. She was in her early eighties at this point, he in his early fifties.

The day was quiet, with few birds, and the pond was almost silent. He and his mother were sitting in the backyard after he had returned from doing some international traveling for work. To rest, he was reading to her the *New York Times* extended obituary on the life and work of Erik Erickson.

As he was explaining the difference between Erickson's view of multiple journeys in life and the Freudian presumption of one big identity crisis, she said, "I have had six identity crises in my life." He paused in astonishment. Not a single cloud interrupted what came next.

"First when your father died, then when your sister left to get married, and then again when you left for Cornell." What came after that, he hardly had to ask. "I felt what Erickson meant when my brother moved out to Albuquerque, when your Uncle Ziggy died, and then when I began to lose my mobility."

She knew that he had read the works of Sigmund Freud, whom she hated. That afternoon, she aligned her stars with Erickson. "Do not forget, Bruce, you wrote your dissertation about Walt Whitman because the father you never knew was called Walt."

A FUNERAL
MESSAGE

Lillian loved this Long Island church—as much as she loved the sounds and smells of her home in West Islip.

The simple joys of her life were her saints, her meals, and her pleasantly unique conversations. She was like Walt Whitman all over again when at the Robert Moses beach—all happy and clear, most days. And like Walt, she saw meaning in death.

During the funeral ceremony, his sister Terry wrote heartfelt comments that by chance echoed Caedmon, without knowing it. She read: "Now let us praise the Guardian of the Kingdom of Heaven, the might of the Creator and the thought of His mind, the work of the glorious Father, how He, the eternal Lord, established the beginning of every wonder."

When Terry spoke, he felt the "He" she was referring to was Lillian, their culturally ignored but great mother. As an athlete, he knew there was something deviant in thinking of the heavenly feminine, yet he also felt that she hovered over her family like a heavenly body. Without stern punishment, without much education, she had ensured that her children would remain under moral rule, and learn how to tame both the beasts around them and the beasts ticking in their hearts. Lillian did all this with little direct power and few resources. During her funeral, this growing awareness overwhelmed him. "What force granted her so much grace?" he began to ask—a discussion he carried with him for some time.

Since Lillian's death, whenever he visited Westminster Abbey and sat thinking of her, he felt best beneath the memorial to Oliver Goldsmith. The back door to this often-ignored part of the abbey leads to St. Faith's Chapel, a hideaway chapel far from the throngs of people peering in at the popular entrance. And it was there, in this small chapel, after all these centuries of war, and under the words of the Oliver Goldsmith memorial, that he could sit in private prayer—without God, without dogma, simply with the sound and strong memories of his mother.

His mind goes there whenever he thinks of his mother. She is there, somewhere in the abbey. She is there—everywhere—in literature. She is always there, his Missing Person.

COASTAL BLISS
EXISTS

He thanked God for seashells. When feeling generous, he even thanked the Long Island beaches where shells were found—free, adorable, and awaiting his hands. But he came to thank his wife even more.

Since his childhood, he had found great relief in looking through the Golden Nature guide *Seashells of the World*. Years later and far from the sea, he still had that $1.25 edition in his home office. He cherished this small book.

Yet his most amazing find, his shell of shells, was his wife, Varlissima: a woman who contained all women. In the course of his life, he would come to believe there was something special and historic in a composite. Varlissima herself embodied these higher facts. If there was any lasting meaning in the word "supernatural," it had to do with these formations of composites in his life, starting with Varlissima. She was part his mother, part his early lovers, yet completely herself.

Varlissima was at times as dark as the olive shells of Africa; at other times, she was white, with the shape and spin of a tulip shell. For him, watching her eyebrows was blissful, pure joy.

Variety was the essence of Varlissima, a most passionate woman. Shakespeare could write about his dark lady and about his fair youth, but he would write about Varlissima, the woman who knew the oceans would rise years before the warning became real.

Her hand gestures, her raised eyebrows, her changeable smile proved alarming and more worthy than the simple shells of his youth. The heart and soul of Varlissima, this bright vegetarian from Yonkers, was pure energy to this ex-athlete. And the tension in being near her was always tender and alert.

His coaches had said the same thing about basketball, but Varlissima was saying it about their life. This changed his sense of self, and his sense of purpose all at once.

She said the profound in the shape of disarming jokes. "Why were men given larger brains than dogs?" she once asked him at Sapsucker Woods outside the Cornell campus. "So they will not hump a woman's legs during the start of a cocktail party!" "Why does it take one million sperm to fertilize a female egg? Sperm refuse to stop and ask for directions."

For years, he would walk with Varlissima—miles at a time, sometimes a dozen in a day—trying to calm her, hoping for calm in her. He wanted to hear that whisper again, the oceans within her. It often proved difficult.

In his memory, she remained troubled, as if in a storm. This was part of her appeal, something only sex seemed to calm for the few first decades. Varlissima was the rage of Italian oceans, the chill outside each Roman *pensione* they strove to share.

Thirty years later, she still remembered how cold she had been the night she walked with him and a few friends to Midnight Mass on Christmas Eve in Venice. In her he sensed the inevitability of flooding in San Marco.

She remained a shell of shells, full of variety, full of the charm of surprise, and the force of a storm. Between them remained a space, a difference of immense consequence and certain closeness.

TRIPS TO SICILY

The massive chank shell, with its smooth, glasslike curve, is found in a few parts of the world, mostly Ceylon and India. But, like the best of anything, it is traded widely. He had one on his desk when he first met his future wife. Nervously, as he was eyeing her shape, her smile, sensing his longing, and hers, he would look to the chank shell on that desk, to relieve some tension.

He had heard that in India, chank shells are collected by ambitious women, who cut them into ornamental rings and bangles. From the start, he felt Varlissima's ambition and she felt his. Sometimes left-handed chank shells—genetic defects—can be found on Hindu altars, mounted in gold. He felt the same way about Varlissima: she was a rare one indeed. The slant of light in the afternoon mounted her in gold. He would become a writer, and a businessman of some impact, if he could have her with him as he grew.

Yet they still had massive differences, differences larger than the seas between Sicily and the rest of Italia, full of sirens and myths, rich with fog and swift currents.

There must be a happier middle ground, he thought, between the strength of her seas and the wants of his loins, between the smart poverty of her thoughts and his taking off her pants. This was his internal argument for decades, being half a centaur, and half a very practical businessman. It was the tension between them that was supreme—but, unlike most supreme things, this tension lasted decades.

Sicily's seaside resort of Taormina was built on Mount Tauro in the fourth century before Christ, by exiles from the nearby Greek colony of Naxos, who merged happily with the local populations. This was clearly a part of their genius, this easy merging with folks quite opposite. The town first became famous in the 1700s, when rich young Europeans included it in their grand tour after college. By the time he and Varlissima arrived at Taormina, it was a tourist destination with international sparkle and intrigue. So walking up the steps to the theater of Taormina with Varlissima fit properly, in a primal archeological way. Whenever he was depressed about her stubbornness, he'd recall each of the many worn stone steps leading up to the theater, where the sound was supreme, and the view closer to heaven than anything he had ever seen.

The birds were hers, and the shorelines, and the steep rock steps. She was the world of Sicily by his side, and he loved that very much.

Life is always more important than work, she made him see at last.

The Greek Theatre of Segesta in Sicily's province of Trapani is a perfect semicircle. This space offered them a generous panorama, exactly as dictated by the rules of ancient design.

As they walked along the beach, Varlissima would enrich the hike with intriguing idioms from around the world.

Remembering their time at the Temple della Concordia, where one of the best-preserved temples of Greek antiquity in Sicily sits, he recalled that the temple had been converted into a Christian church in the sixth century. That is what, ironically, had safeguarded it from the normal neglect and destruction. Knowing this history, he figured out ways to keep Varlissima from the known harms and wrongs of time.

Like Lillian, Varlissima had her own magical way of refocusing his native competitiveness to make it less warlike when at home. She was educating him, making him ready for the ultimate gift of fathering Colette.

The hilarious underbelly beneath all their outward anger was inward love. It was their great differences and close intimacy that helped him sidestep self-destruction. They both shared a youth of poverty and books, a time of severe and liberating discoveries at Cornell, and many sweet evenings together. That was enough to keep them near each other for life.

One Sunday morning in Potsdam, where they had landed their first after-college jobs at Clarkson University, in the dead center of St. Lawrence County, she had given him two black eyes. It happened when she lifted her knees as he gingerly bounced back to bed on a very frigid North Country morning. The sound of his eyes quashing was something he never forgot. She left town the next day for a week of work elsewhere—a rare happening during those North Country days—so he had to quickly make up a story about his black eyes to protect his pride before seeing his students and his fellow ball players at the Clarkson gym. He claimed that the black eyes had resulted when a vindictive ballplayer responded to his head fake with double elbows.

Nothing was important enough for him to leave Varlissima—the incredible finely scripted letters he would find everywhere when he woke early, her meticulous kitchen notes about how she'd end the relationship if he left another coffee grind near her breakfast. He was in a double bind, and he came to like it. He wrote her extended letters of refutation during his travels but would not send them, mostly because he came to see them as stupid when he returned home.

For him, it was all about the coasts, and for her, it was all about the oceans. He suspected that it was this balancing calm that had attracted the volatile and ever-electric Varlissima to him in the first place—her eyebrows expressing urgent need, her legs jumpy to move or to be pinned down again. She once slipped in a warning to a new swimming mate: "If you really want a committed man, pick the best-dressed one in the mental hospital."

Despite their dramatic differences, their love and marriage would last more than half a century, and he somehow knew that during these early walks.

A MADDENING
COUPLE

They made a maddening couple to friends, who claimed they embodied opposites. "Opposites attract," his loving biological sister Terry would often say. She was the meat in the shell, and he was the shell. He was the aggressor. She was one of the infinites who absorbed his aggression. She was becoming him, and he was becoming her. He could live with this tension; Mr. and Mrs. Tolstoy had. In fact, he used his sense of couple-hood to hide some personal and spiritual crises, and that felt good. She was the ocean, and he remained coastal in his bliss.

As they walked the long, skeletal coasts of southwest Sicily, they paused, hand in hand, to view the majestic waves, to feel the heat, and to breathe in the salty air. It was only the two of them there—before the discovery of Colette—and it was there that they never resolved their differences, and it was there that they became resolved.

One walks the earth alone or with a keen other. He found his keen other in Varlissima. Yet still she remained troubled, a woman stirred like a top of ceaseless emotion. He could eat a steak. Take a long nap. Awake to find her looking lovely—and exactly like her volatile self, reading, but not calm.

The more she talked, the more her hair made sense to him.

It was large hair, and red. Her soft voice made many youthful narratives in his mind. He wanted, so badly, to capture the essence of that voice to share it whenever he could. Otherwise, he feared it might disperse, like the misty memories of his father. After many decades with this wife, he started to write about their youth, and about his immense longing during their days with their daughter.

Together they began to recall the many missing persons who had visited their home. Writing their recollections was his way of honoring those who were gone.

Unexpectedly, this coupling of fear and joy with her enabled him to become even more appreciative of the valor in women.

PREGNANT AND UNCHANGING

By the age of forty-two, he knew he could no longer contain a woman like Varlissima. "Strong women contain too much flooding," he thought. For him, this meant becoming more than an academic, and embracing a life of action.

Varlissima told him that the seas would rise up against his coasts, and that someday all men would perish from this earth. And with that she said, "Yes! Yes!" she would marry him.

The marriage took place in Saratoga Springs on Broadway at Cafe Panini restaurant. To perform the ceremony, they employed a Unitarian female minister, something not easy to find so near the six million acres of the Adirondack mountains. They were in their home, first built in 1770, a month before the marriage. This was a fine home that had once been burnt down during the French and Indian Wars, but its calming features and its large open expanse were exactly right for them.

Even when pregnant, Varlissima was amazing—walking, cooking, talking, being Varlissima. Some women are paused by the size and weight of childbearing. Varlissima found it liberating. He saw that he and Varlissima could not, should not, stop walking as a couple; for if they did, they might forfeit their confidence, and never again regain respect for each other. They took long walks up to the hour before Colette was born on August 29, 1996. From that moment on, he knew that he would need to learn to appreciate Varlissima for what she was. That was a big part of coastal bliss.

The more she talked, the more he came to understand her hair. With the birth of Colette, he was now ready to leave teaching.

With the birth of Colette, he threw himself into the money-making aspects of being a consultant hired from his books. While still an academic, teaching at Rensselaer's Lally School of Management and Technology, he was earning double his academic salary—sometimes triple—each week both teaching and consulting.

Then Toyota gave him a three-year offer to build a six-person team so they could innovate the Prius—and that was so good he could not refuse. He left tenure at RPI, and left all those years of teaching, with a smile. He would now be paid a month's salary for a single talk in France, or Italy, or around the States. It felt too good to be without fear. He brought these fears with him as he consulted in even more complex teams at Merck, Walgreens Boots Alliance, and Walmart.

ile Freud wrote *The Interpretation of Dreams*, he joked, maybe I should write the *Interpretation of Teams*. Most of his new wealth was made by assembling change management teams for global firms. His college roommate, Scot Paltrow, suggested that whimsical title. Instead, he wrote about Michael Jordan, Navy Seals, and Lance Armstrong and called it *Doing More with Teams*. Fantasy of ambition had become fact in that case.

62

FRIDA AND HIS FLY

Yet the juice in joy kept spilling in his direction. Was this real, this flavorful abundance? When he first met Frida, he was glad that she had been dead for nearly sixty years. Otherwise, he might have needed to divorce Varlissima. He had met Frida in an art book. Frida was fabulous because he could not have her.

He was aware that he couldn't technically call her a lover, any more than his friends could call his cigar smoking safe. It was a boyish lie even to call Frida a friend, but it felt good to do so. Self-deception is an element of creation, he believed. That's what he found so pleasant and juicy about good art and good books.

There was a magical certainty in her eyes. In the end, he found that like all great art, she was only wiggling his wants all along, at no real risk to his family. There was a strange torture to her joined eyebrows that pleased him. His tightening pants remained a subject of distraction with her. Frida and his fly seemed connected at the level of his best neurotransmitters, like the words "Madonna" and "Milano" or "Frida" and "fly."

Her paintings made him twiddle with his fly. It did not matter what her husband, Diego, thought. It did not matter that he refused to visit her in Mexico City. She was immense, and immediate, and Frida. Over time, the world would come to see how much she mattered—and for her, that was all that mattered.

She became a colorful orchid in his mind, wet and open and inviting. Her talk in Spanish made him want to hold her delicate neck, fondle her in English, and bring her head near. He was then near joy, near an endless supply of both imagined and focused energy.

Her accented expressions said, "Get closer," after all. He would not be able to resist, even as he aged. Her work would chronically disturb him, as all great art is meant to do.

That was why he was glad he never came across her work in any American museums until he was already committed. And while there was plenty of art in his offices, he never had a piece of Frida's art near. That would be like populating work with pornography, or eating dessert first.

He felt it wise to talk about her as a composite of all his past lovers—mostly to himself, but also to a few dear neighbors and friends who looked at him with longing in their eyes. They knew Varlissima was his answer long before he did.

THE DISCOVERY
OF COLETTE

On the night Colette was born, she looked straight at her father that first second of her life.

She felt at home with his voice; this gave him immense pleasure. Infants need words, just as they need warmth, breast milk, and soft but firm swaddling. He could sense that early on. Yet their need for words is immediate, not deliberate.

Adults need words that can last, like a promise. Children can contemplate a vast immediate.

Colette gave him a new reason to contemplate midlife. She was at once glorious, like fuzzy fiddleheads in April about to burst forth. She walked the weekend before her first year, as if the calendar had been calibrated just for her.

When he looked into her patient eyes, he felt that timing was everything. At forty-two, he was indeed prepared to enjoy childrearing. The ancient Anasazi knew exactly when to plant corn in Chaco Canyon to collect the right amount of sun and rain in the harsh desert light. The birth of Colette was a similar harvest for him and his wife.

Colette was completely herself—and remained that way, to his utter astonishment and stunning satisfaction, forever.

COLETTE AT NIGHT

At night he excelled, thinking through the moves of his next business day. This made most of his days prepared and less vulnerable to the passage of time. Perhaps night work kept him from dreaming, as he struggled to resolve things at night rather than to explore them. His days became delicious this way, but somehow serious and solemn.

When he drew near Colette at night, his long-embedded habits changed. He could hear her breathe—a few ounces of air per breath—and the space of that inhale gave way to a new, less prepared, less decisive, more wondrous world. The next day, his darker side would lift some, or even disappear. Memory was mixed with present joy, and it proved different.

Colette at night was close to wonder. She took away his thoughts about what came next. When he woke the next morning, he didn't feel so much refreshed as remade, like a paragraph of prose that gets reconfigured into a poem, or a phrase from a friend restated as pure unqualified praise.

Later, he would remember this phase vividly, and would understand why less selfish couples created mountains of children to surrender to. Eventually, he came to believe that God had granted Varlissima and him a careful complement.

Colette at night took many things from him, even his health at times, but the exchange of air between them was worth every second from his life.

THE FIRST
OBSESSION

He received tenure at Rensselaer early in life, in the Management School, running his own Master of Science program. But this did not suffice. Reading was his first obsession. Born to disadvantage, but enabled by the grace of good books, reading was to him as basic as breathing. It seldom left his side.

When Colette was about ten, the family had taken a vacation to Portland, Oregon. There, he sat one afternoon with his daughter on a park bench that had at one end, a statue of a seated man: the man was relaxed, his left ankle resting on his right thigh, and he wore a broad-rimmed hat to protect his face from the sun.

But what stuck in his mind, in finding a photograph from that afternoon, was neither the statue nor the park, nor the pleasure of being with his daughter. What he remembered was that on that bench between him and Colette lay a book.

For years afterward, whenever Colette was away, the image of that book sitting between them would haunt him. Why could he not have sat alone with Colette, in a blinding immediacy?

Half the trouble with this reading obsession came from the ways that good reading came to erase obstacles for him. Reading had reshaped the contours of misfortune in his youth, and then outdistanced his self-doubt upon meeting women like Varlissima. Reading was full of symbolic domination.

The other half of this first and lasting obsession was that it could suspend time. Reading was the only tonic that calmed the speed of time for him. As he sat surrounded by pages, engaged in another's narratives, imagining other lives, suddenly decades would pass, and he would emerge more informed with daughter and wife.

Within a year of having received tenure at Clarkson, he discovered that he disliked the stability—and the threat of stability—so much that he left to work for Mario Cuomo's New York State Energy Research and Development Authority, in 1988 and 1989.

Now, without ever having taken a business class in his life, he was a tenured director at the Lally School of Management and Technology. This recognition of his ability to read and to adapt came to haunt him. Once accepted into a club, he often resisted remaining in the club.

And within a year of receiving tenure at Rensselaer, he left again, only to roam more broadly in his readings. During his decade at Rensselaer, he was often simply astonished that management faculty had no real books on their shelves. They had data that aged. This made him realize that he had to leave the academic setting completely for something else, something more action oriented. With that, he had to leave their world for something, anything else. It was the uncertainty of the game that always seduced him to excel, and it was the certainty of academic schedules that frightened him the most.

ATTIC BLISS

His 2007 *World Inc* book was beginning to have him travel the world, as translators brought this investigation in the size of the modern global corporation in a time of social needs into Italian, Greek, Portuguese, Mandarin, Japanese, Korean, and with each new edition came both revenue and consulting to his firm.

He chose to call this writer's paradox, live in an attic bliss. For him, it was the sweet spot outside of writer's block. He was the world in which he walked, and what he heard and made came from his home, his origins. And yet what he stored in the attic of his soul was proving shareable and valued. Memory is a kind of accomplishment. He knew this best from the attic of their home on Old Stone Church Road. In the litter of that attic, he saw everything he had accomplished, and all that he had not. He had some of his best thoughts in that attic, and a few of his worst.

Varlissima had encouraged him to look at dozens of properties before they settled on the white home across from the Old Stone Church. There were dozens of problems with the property, from the flood in the basement to the insects in the attic. But the place spoke to both of them instantly—and they knew that it was lifelong, and they knew it would be a challenge to maintain and improve.

The house was on an ancient site, pre-Revolutionary, from the time of the French and Indian War. It was near a pond, with more than a dozen giant maples lining the old carriage route to the Old Stone Church, which was across the street. Most importantly, it was the place where Colette was born, and then grew up.

Colette had now lived in the home for a dozen years. Much time had passed, while she did archery in the backyard and became a talented athlete. It was already August, and she was about to turn into a teenager before their eyes.

Yet time itself was suspended in the attic: layers of dust dated the gifts. He could remember her complete past, and now worried about her near future.

The rocking chair—that strange, horse-like rocking chair that Colette would ride on for hours—was still there, in the slanted light of the attic. Her Christmas gifts seemed antiques, eyeing her new interests, so suddenly arrived.

Suddenly, he felt he saw two girls from his attic view, each pausing at the window of her bedroom. One was innocence itself; the other stood tall, like a young woman with a bearskin on her skull, like the ancient god Artemis herself. The first, slightly stooped, was nameless and without precedent, seeking safety and security, humbled yet somehow also proud.

Old Stone Church was to the left of this girl's choice, with open, pine-filled woods to the right. He could see both girls in the one girl, and this worried him.

One jumps into the future, and this Colette is lovely in motion, certain in motion, running like a deer, like a reborn Artemis, bow in hand, ready to accept a college scholarship for such balance in running. This is the Colette we can have confidence in. She makes the fall safely into life, matures like the rest of us, and settles well each night into sleep.

But there is another Colette, suspended in her fall, arrested in the worst sense, motionless in the air. And while she is embraced by her father, she is not free to be herself.

She is in pinched quarters like a servant.

She is in a garret, like a struggling artist.

She is in a room for a lonely child.

She is in a sanctum without noise and family.

She is behind time, and alone.

She is an image from another life.

This second Colette wrote a letter to Emily Dickinson, who never wrote back to her.

MIDDLEBURY, VERMONT

Now fifty-three, having watched the self-destruction of so many talented as well as so many disadvantaged people, he concluded that it is not boastful to think of yourself as great when you yourself outsmart poverty. By fifty-three, he had written a *New York Times* bestseller from a state of mind that was his own—how to do more with less. This was his ninth book in thirty years, and it would not prove to be his last.

During the prior decade, he was leaving the art of writing in black and white, and started trying more colorful things. Blending fiction and nonfiction in his books on business and society was beginning to feel right, and some readers were responding.

Greatness resides in each of us, if tapped with diligence, allowing the developed self to defeat the destructive self.

When he looked over so much self-destruction in the lives of creative people in the past, he felt lucky—even at times, great—to have found someone who was a sound family man, and a creative man to boot. Yet in meeting his writer-mentor friend Jay Parini, it came together in a way that served his ambition, his family, and his love of fine literature.

Without having met Jay Parini, however, he would most likely have remained arrested in his own attic of hope and rusted intentions. He needed a writer as a mentor near his fears. Not just agents and publishers, but real writers, who knew what it took and took it all very well.

He met Jay in a moment of sudden rightness, when Colette wasn't yet a woman, and when he was ripe with business, but not yet ripe enough to write about his own life.

Jay lived on top of a hill outside Middlebury, Vermont, ninety-three miles from the Old Stone Church. He had discovered Jay's books by chance. He had been flipping through the racks of Lyrical Ballad, a used bookstore on Phila Street in Saratoga. He picked up a book by Jay that reminded him of greatness. And this used bookstore gave him Jay for less than five bucks.

That same month Jay called him to ask about what it was like to do a dissertation under the leadership of M. H. Abrams.

After having seen one of Jay's novels made into a fine independent movie, he boldly sent him his new manuscript, which was about Ben Franklin and the art of competitive frugality. He included a short letter praising Jay's film, *The Last Station*, and its tale about two loves: one between a young man and woman, and the other between Tolstoy and his wife—an old lion and his lioness. Jay invited him in. The trip into Jay's world became a routine. Writer to writer, friend to friend.

In reaching Jay's world, he relearned how to leave his world of professional distractions and inconsequential distinctions.

In meeting Jay, he came to a moment of reconciliation with his own ambition. He was ordinary, and that was enough. He lived a writer's life, with mounting financial success—and that was special. The way forward was to articulate this ordinary specialness that all humans share.

HIS NEIGHBORHOOD

After meeting Jay, he became again a literary frontiersman.

The Old Stone Church, originally a jolly good investment, was now igniting his imagination. Backed by his finances as a management consultant, and taking the extra cash from the sales of his books, he had bought the old place, with its church, and his home, and the large Adirondack rooms, and the immense, ready-to-fall barn, at a bargain-basement price.

The giant maples that lined the ancient carriage way to the church began to astonish him. Almost the entire time he had been a professor, he had not taken the time to walk that part of the property.

It was the same now for his trips; he brought the library of his literary ambitions with him on the road now. He hired Ed, a local archeologist and another friend he met through books, to dig around in his basement, and sure enough it was pre-Revolutionary. The basement could be clearly dated to 1770, perhaps to the early 1760s, making it older than all the other stock in Saratoga, including the Old Brian Inn.

He was feeling more a part of history than ever before. From the Old Stone Church, up through central Vermont, he would drive past land mines of memories.

"Be open to the sun," he heard them say.

"Be bolder," he heard Jay say.

Visiting Jay, this American narrative writer, brought a storm of longings back to him: his education, his desire to write new things, the things of his youth that had been neglected during his moneymaking years. Boom. All back.

He recalled Henry David Thoreau's breathtaking encounter with the loon, and he thought he could try to write more boldly now, beyond the reach and needs of his agents.

After meeting Jay, his neighborhood became as rich as his hand-selected library. He knew now, after meeting Tom Wolfe, how you could be entertaining and informative, delightful and persuasive. He began to write in color about business and society, not separately. Tom Wolfe and Gay Talese and a few others at The Lotos Club in Manhattan pointed this out to him in his books. It had been there all along, but in recognizing it more explicitly the writer's life began to emerge above and beyond the businessman.

He said to Varlissima, "I guess self-delusion can be such a good thing. It allows the writer a chance at a more inclusive style, a bigger grab at meaning. For after tons of trying as a specialist, you become an accepted generalist. As a writer, you develop the skills of a more daily self-invention!"

MOBY DICK AND THE COLOR WHITE

He was now in his middle fifties. How had that happened? He picked up Melville again to see a path forward.

After so much preparation, after so much reading, he now knew the answers were in studying the great writers. Without uttering a single word, Jay, through all of his published words collectively, helped him accept his standing, and proceed as both writer and businessman.

He'd look out his office window at the hanging sculpture of a copper whale from the New Bedford Whaling Museum swaying in the wind, so bright it would shed reflected light. It reminded him daily of how great Melville was to his mind.

He had taught for seven years at Clarkson "the Great Books curriculum"—Aurelius to Franklin, Whitman, and Melville. Those days spent teaching the greats were a blip compared to now, when he could consume a classic without needing to tell anyone.

Rereading these classics now, away from Cornell, long gone from Potsdam and Troy, was pure pleasure. Marquez's magical *One Hundred Years of Solitude*, the great literature of reality by Tom Wolfe and Gay Talese, the strong histories by Robert Caro—each brought new techniques to his page. He was, at last, preparing himself for a still larger literary world.

Nonetheless, with some strangeness, and that same remorse from poverty in youth, each hour that he spent with a master classic, he felt like he was getting away with murder. He had been trained, born to be a laborer, so this leisure-class pleasure was, in the back of his mind, still perverse. This perversity was a cause of guilt, and the guilt was deeper than guilt, since it involved remorse.

Fate had allowed him so much more: he could sway in the wind like that copper whale.

The story line becomes sublime. The setting makes the ordinary extraordinary.

This deeper sense of self in every reader is neither coastal nor oceanic, neither rich nor poor. It is universal. It is sublime. It is inclusive. It is like an apricot: sensual, made of curls and curves, made to delight.

In this passage he felt all the seasons of Melville's mind. Yet the chapter did not move forward: it was not based on a protagonist, and did not relate at all to Ahab or Ishmael. The chapter stood on its own: self-contained, magnificent and worthy of occupation. The passage brought him back to that first moment he saw Colette.

Right then and there, he came to understand that Melville had written about white in all its contrasting magnificence. Melville's white was different from, but exactly like, a young girl's face. It was the white of his daughter's face. It was a white of standing in a life.

Life is richest when interrupted, when the colors of life are neither exaggerated nor muted, but exact. The baby cries, the milk spills, the knees scrape. Being attentive to the unaccomplished is its own form of richness.

THE BEACH WHERE
HE WAS BORN

The beach where he was born and the beach where he became a man were one and the same: the Robert Moses Beach Three on Long Island.

However old he became, his memories of those beach days were always golden, always solid. It was here that he never felt alone, as the endlessly shifting sands were his own.

It was here that his fears disappeared during long walks along the coast, as if personal harms were fiction and the story line of his life was mostly and essentially good.

There could be a thousand others near his side, but he could still feel content at his beach. It was here that he brought Varlissima at her charming best, his daughter Colette at her finest, his mother, and his muses. The beach never disappointed them—seldom left them with a dark impression, despite brutal storms and fierce ocean winds.

The salt on his face was saving. Here he met the wind, caressed the surf, chased with stern gestures the terns and other coastal birds until they looked at him with idle suspicion, heads tilted sideways and legs readied for flight.

Urged on by the music of the beach, by its simple cadence, he shared the same breath with the beach. It was the beach where he was born, after all; the beach where he remained a man.

In youth he concluded that a beach was more his library, and that the surf and the wind were his most whimsical friends.

Part Two

THE SENSUAL MIDDLE

(VIGNETTES OF EXPERIENCE AND MIDDLE AGE)

*"I have acquired very few notions only on what is
better not to put in a book. Paint only what
you have seen. Look for a long time at those things
that give you pleasure, still longer at those
things that give you pain. Try to be faithful to your
first impression. Don't make a fetish of
the 'rare word.' Don't tire yourself with lying."*

—Colette

THE ART OF BEING A DOG

In 2014, he gave a reading at the NorthShire bookstore in Manchester, Vermont. It proved clarifying for both his identity and his reputation. It was an alert grouping of people, and he remembered how cold the marble stones were outside the front door, and how warm he became in the act of being himself. It was there that he found a perspective on his writer's life.

He had once known a dog named Zachary. Zach would limp for affection and attention. He might be sniffing the ground, but he was always eyeing something better. Zach was a fantastic dog, warm and fuzzy, smart and tenacious.

Nonetheless, he was easily distracted by a new smell or a new thought; even squirrels could instantly change his calculating equation—and he'd sprint off, forgetting the limp that had gotten him noticed in the first place.

In youth—and even in middle age—there were so many ways in which he felt like Zach, felt himself exactly like a dog. For years, he thought this was because he had come into the world poor, with little advantage except his senses and wit, but now he knew better.

Colette thought that her dad-man had been a bear in another life, "because you protect your cubs, and because you are big and cuddly." Not really, he thought—the deeper, less romantic truth was that he was a dog. No adults really felt him to be a bear, and while he loved his young Artemis daughter, he felt that she exaggerated his size and reach.

His animal spirit was reflective of his deep nature. What was funny was that they, the public, kept feeding him, prompting him. Opponents on the basketball court, whenever he caught them in a fake, called him a dog; early business partners, like Robin, who had owned paintings by Rembrandt, paused when he'd bought them out, to call him a dog. When he met his investors' obligations and left the world of debt before age forty, some had called him un-American—but most had called him, behind his back, "another white Cornell-bred dog." They were usually from the better breed of schools like Harvard, INSEAD, the London School of Economics, or the Manchester School of Business—and their deans and faculty had come from similar pedigrees. He took no offense; but as he did on the basketball court, he chose to make their offense the object of his skill.

Why had it taken him so many decades to accept the obvious? God had granted him a dog's curiosity since his birth in that home near the railroad tracks. Nothing more, little less. Yet it was nothing short of hilarious and gracious and good that the big men and the big women in society kept rewarding him for being dog-like. At church, a minister asked that the social progressives in his community become like boa constrictors—"We need you to be bold, open, and affirmative! Amen! That is our calling in life. Be a boa—offer yourself to a life of action for the good."

Bruce felt that the metaphor of being a good dog was much more convincing. He was afraid to tell his minister this. He knew to go with what interested him, until something even better roamed before him. Having survived a rather turbulent youth, he thought: "You can always go back to the original smells, and find a place to leave your mark."

He began thinking that the good deals that had granted him privilege had resided somewhere in his brain before they became real. This was his most fascinated thought since the birth of his daughter—spunk was in him all along, and it was about learning to let it out. Many spoke of the importance of self-esteem, others about self-worth, and a few more missionaries harped about the certainty of wealth as a sign of divine obligation. This all seemed a bit elevated in his mind, for he knew business to be pedestrian, and success a collection of white scattered bones.

Dante taught him that most lives are more a divine comedy than some stately sequence. His position between the inferno of self-interest and the hells of business and literary accomplishment were punctuated by many adventures in realms of more pleasant, heavenly things, such as the smile of a girl or the chase of a dog in the park. Each peak of pleasure seemed to matter more as he aged, and memories came in the scent of a woman, in the muddy trail of a deal, in running so fast that he sometimes ran right over the petrified squirrels he was chasing.

Memory was stored like the smells in a dog—by intensity, by category, and in a vast and complex system of recall.

After the discovery of Colette, he began to dig deeper, sniffing around a bit, to see what was still out there.

THE SENSUAL
CERTAINTY OF YOUTH

While enjoying, from joy to joy, occasional receptions of his writing, it was business that inflamed most days. Business was this moth, his moth, a serious yellow-tailed moth, with large green eyes on its wings. This moth of serious distraction flapped its zigzag ways into consuming a life, his life, much of his middle life, as it gave him a sense of mission, a purpose, a stage that seemed to grow each night, expand each city, evolve into a global exchange.

A business-based day proved much easier than the anxiety inherent in fine writing. He would use his classes to entertain himself and the students with some of his findings, but he would use his life to profit from the learning. The moth kept growing in its intensities.

Why is this fitting? Well, when you grow up poor, it is nearly impossible to resist the moth. Have you ever noticed how hilarious even the best dogs look when running to chomp down a moth? In retrospect, looking over his decades in business, he could now see himself in that posture, a dog ready to chomp down the next moth. Month after month, the next moth hovers. Opportunity is sweet, and she is a self-consuming clown's assistant.

Daily, his eyes would track the moth when you look up; stupidity is trying to kill the moth. He began to ease off some from his chase, but when he realized this, he had already run through much of the world.

Oddly, as if in a bad joke, he, the born reader and born egotist, was becoming more social. His failings were the failures of humanity, not just his own. It was no longer fair for him to fault himself for being too impersonal. His business success in Africa and Canada depended clearly on the persistence of these attributes. How was all this travel and work even possible?

For the one truly beautiful thing about most dogs is that they are not distracted by endless horizons; they know and want home. Now he saw it as part of Edwin's culture, his integration back into Puerto Rico, and understood enough to forgive Edwin. He felt the foolishness now, his foolishness and pride, not Edwin's. There was this strange acceptance in review.

He remembered vividly when Suie Yin Chang left for adoption in California. The sudden feeling of change for Terry, his sister, was overwhelming. Terry cried several Sundays in a row at church. He felt helpless again. Not many families experience the loss of so many children, a father, and a grandmother. And all this—in the first fifteen years of life! He would meet many competitors in his life, but only a few had this kind of training. It was an understatement to call this street smarts. A writer's life is built on these stones of fear and longing, mixed by a cement called joy.

The missing persons of his life were now taking on certainty. They were the certainty of his survival, the benefits in the risks he took daily now, in bigger and bigger leagues, with larger and larger returns. In youth, risks seemed to invade his mind. In middle age, they seemed to explain his mind, and his hungry behaviors.

He remembered again his last day with his father . . . and when Lillian left him for good so suddenly. He remembered the phone call from Terry that Lillian was dying. The anxious flight to Florida only to find her gone. These events still pained him. He built his books on top of these pains.

PULA, CROATIA

Colette in Croatia sounded right, far better than her first study choice in dengue fever rich parts of Africa. While feeling full of a father's fears, he accepted Croatia like he accepted her inevitable growth spurts. She was a gift to the world now, and not within his control. She had jumped the coop, left her Saratoga chickens behind, and the weight of that home's attic.

Before becoming a pre-med student in Ithaca College, Colette selected a summer in Croatia. She chose a program in Pula, down the spit of land from Italy's Trieste. She allowed Varlissima and her father to visit the first week to settle in. He never forgot Croatia, its coastal bliss of a thousand small islands. He felt joy near the Arch of Sergius in Pula, the Roman section.

When he watched her talk in Croatia in the Scaletta hotel restaurant, his joy and pride jumped all over his fatherly fears. Not but three short blocks from the lovely

Pula Harbor, at the tip of the Peninsula that had lasting military value to the Roman navy for centuries, this small Pavillion-based restaurant hotel was the best they could afford of the East and the West, while visiting Colette that week. The basilica, a Roman Colosseum full of music, the Roman amphitheater—these were not big enough to contain her clear openness to it all.

It is funny how a good set of meals, and a walk, alleviate fear, that stupid toy.

Colette was studying medicine as an intern with a class of sophisticated international peers all gathered by three British doctors in a group. Some might call this group more a gang for good. He found the doctors celebratory, despite the profound ailments of the populace they served. And Colette found her peers preciously interesting.

One came from Moscow, another from Istanbul, a third from London. Scaletta was selected as one of the seven best havens for food in Istria. It specialized in Italian dishes, but also offered him fine coffees in the early morning, and some ancient culinary treats for desserts. His fear abated, as he got into some Slavic spice and mystery.

He remembered how European the young female student from Moscow appeared, as they chatted, in an unhurried ambience of pizza, seafood, and Bavarian beer. He now had proof that the new world would be approached by his daughter through medicine.

HIS FATHER GLIMPSED
IN ISTANBUL

That day in Turkey was misty. The Bosporus let off steam as it had on the day that Constantinople had first fallen, in 1453. The hairs on his arms were standing, electric, as if a storm would soon be joining the steam.

He was in Istanbul on one of his many business trips. He had been there often enough not to get lost in the seven hills. There was something fresh in Istanbul's union of East and West—something forgiving, cluttered with opposites, and beautiful. He sensed in Istanbul, as he did in Africa, that he was in a part of the world that was on the rise.

He had been sitting at an outdoor cafe doing some paperwork, when suddenly he caught a glimpse of a man coming out of a shop who looked exactly like his father.

In a near-hypnotic state, he gathered up his papers and began following this man, who reminded him so much of his dad. As he walked behind him, he began to reminisce, remembering how much he missed his father. In actuality, he had spent less time with his dad than he had with many of his business associates. But now, he projected intense feelings associated with his father onto this observed stranger—imagining the way he talked and even the way he walked these seven hills.

Even the posture of this man said, "You're going to miss me when I'm gone." Bruce could almost hear him whispering this remorse in English. "I've taken the high road in this short life," and "I know it must hurt you, Bruce, that I am so remote. But you have done a good job of looking for me—and fathering yourself."

This trip had taught him something about his longing for his father and about his home. For years, every man in a military uniform had reminded him of the uniforms in his father's attic. The strange World War II medals— the confusing awards for serving in the Pacific—were anointed by the oils of his fingertips. The absolute silence of relatives, except when talking about rank and the larger mission, began to bother him, even when he was in places like Turkey. These things made him wonder what his father was really like.

In the end, the only evidence he had was military evidence—damn it; he had never found anything more personal than that. But here in Istanbul, the look in the man's brown eyes was the look of his father's eyes. Before the man disappeared into the crowd, he said once more, "You will miss me when I am gone, even when I am young, even when you are old."

This proved one of the most enjoyable and forgiving memories of his middle years. There was no blame in meeting his father.

A missing father can become a perfect father: without harm, without wrongs, full of feelings.

THE JUMP TO
JAPAN

With his father now settled in his mind, he began to ask a deeper set of questions about his life.

He did this from when his *World Inc* book won a book-of-the-year award in Japanese. No one, really, in America, except his Toyota clients in Torrance, California, and in Manhattan even noticed this award. The book kept jumping into foreign editions, yet the Japanese retained his teams the longest. His jump to Japan brought new fears, anxiously feeling his differences from their group think and patterns of alignment and respect. He would jump for a decade through these hoops, from New York to Torrance, then to Erlinger, then to Japan and back.

He had taken many flights to Japan, China, and Hong Kong for both business and pleasure. He had toured places in the Far East and the southern hemisphere, like Costa Rica and its neighboring sisters, for equal and engaging reasons. These trips built into a set of recurrent patterns, a deeper sense of purpose, but it was during the trips to Asia that this sense of soul searching really stood out.

He began to ask why the artist in him, something he had repressed for business pleasures for so long, continued to work throughout his life rather secretly, rather furtively, and then bloomed in public in his later years. He felt it vividly with each return to Japan, where every inch has been framed, designed, made into art.

This much he knew: He knew he and Varlissima were late bloomers in terms of their devotion to themselves and to family. This strange devotion to the craft and art of writing was not how he was perceived by most of his friends, business partners, and clients for decades, nor was it how he and Varlissima thought of themselves. They were the son and daughter of laborers. Bruce thought of himself, in particular, more as a wordsmith in action, a facilitator of events, of impact, not texts. He thought of his books as contracts, not art.

He started to notice that, silently, across decades, he and Varlissima had brought the art of his travels back into their home, and into his places of work. He first noticed this one day when staring at a small bronze statue of a deer that stood on the mantel over his office fireplace. The deer's proud stance reminded him of what was best in Colette, and what might prove best in him.

This rediscovery took dominion everywhere in his life, like that proud deer on the mantel. He now felt it the divine compensation for having grown up so poor. He was trained to inspect with driven eyes and cheap tools the nature of things free before him. It was the art in a flower, or a friend, or a lover that defined him, not the pretense or the artifact. He did not need to get deeply involved with things that exercised his talents of observation and delight. He acted within like an artist, without like a businessman. This was possible with Japanese businessmen, so why not bring that atmosphere home?

Turning fifty-six, he reread Marguerite Wildenhain's *The Invisible Core*, her book on pottery published in 1976 and reviewed by him at Cornell, when he last felt himself an artist. Besides E. F. Schumacher's *Small Is Beautiful*, he felt this a life-directing book, found at the right key pivot point in his life, and offering a journey that helped him to reconcile his early ambitions and the world. He could recite, throughout life and in the many classes he taught, word by word this passage that meant so much to him:

> *There is no reason to be proud of whatever gifts one has. They are by the grace of God and not the results of our merits. But there is reason to be deeply grateful for them, and this gives one the responsibility to use these gifts to the utmost. And not only for ourselves. The more capacity a person has, the greater and more cogent will be the moral obligation to do something honorable with what he has . . .*
>
> *Let us look at the implication. Man, like all animals, is by nature lazy, but the creative man would always work. He works not only because he wants to create, but because he unconsciously acknowledges his ability to do so with the acceptance of deeper human*

*responsibility. He understands that his work-time can-
not be what it is for most men, from a certain hour to
another definite hour. His work hours will be his total
life, no less. That he feels to be the least he can do to
make up for the gift of abilities that he was given.*

He felt this to be the best passage on divine compensation he ever came across in prose. All the others, and
there were many, he had come across at the theatre, or
in poems, or during speeches he had witnessed by good
fortune—and they were therefore more difficult to share
with the same businesslike exactness. Although he had
never met Wildenhain, he understood what she meant by
devotion. He had always felt devoted.

While living on the opposite side of the world from
Japan, he understood in time their repressed joys and their
relentless ambitions to wander in restrained wonder in
this world. He knew he was both animal and man, both
American and global. The translations of his book *World
Inc* helped this set of new appreciated feelings mature in
the writer, as their checks sat well in his bank.

FORGIVENESS IS THE JOURNEY

He hung a deep-black wooden African mask near his front office door. That was long ago, but he still stood near it a few seconds upon his entry to work each day. The door was magnificent, with long thin sheets of window from top to bottom on each side, so he had a great view of the outside from the inside. But he chose to hang the mask just inside the door, like a hidden totem, so people would be able to see it only upon entry. This way, he could contemplate the darkness of ancient ways before he met another day at his computer. This dark energy was what had settled continents.

The dark African mask assumed some real power in his office. It suggested that he might be able to reach his reset button again, to pretend again that the day was completely new. But he knew he had been transformed by Varlissima once again. It wasn't completely his life, no matter how self-centered he had feigned to be.

Transfiguration was the right word, and it fixed his many wrongs. It enabled him to walk on stilts in the muck of his actual life, skipping through the worst thickets into a smoldering realm of higher fact.

Was this the same kind of mental dance that the ancients had found useful in ritual dramas? At least half of his library collection had been assembled to answer this question about ritual and history.

Some 5,000 years ago, when the last of the men and women had crossed the frigid Bering Strait to a lush new world, had they relied on the same set of skills in order to survive the harsh elements of their crossing?

There were two further lessons in this experience turned transfiguration. By middle life, he had found that the hippocampus and the neocortex are merely the well-paid handlers of the mind, the PR professionals of the self. They do everything they can to justify, to rationalize, as we say.

However, he chose in this case not to overpay, and overplay, these PR pros. He would not allow these pulses to be framed as a midlife crisis. That was too cheap, too easy, too ready-made, too prefabricated. He chose to call the experience behind the church his "Hamlet moment," when he had everything, but that in having everything, he was reminded he had so little left.

He developed a new thought path, similar to the faith first found in Hurricane Sandy, but this time much deeper, more fanciful, best expressed as a lecture in anthropology. This lesson was mostly narrated in dream time:

"Man was born in Africa roughly 50,000 years ago, the genetic record confirms." He felt this dream in narrative form, as if he were watching a PBS documentary on the journey of men . . .

"Small bands of humans then walked to Australia, where the Ice Age froze them into huddles. They huddled tight for eons, sharing skins, but they then were forced across the seas of Indonesia by foot." "The fossil records show," Varlissima notes at this point in the dream, her voice sharper than usual, "that women were critical to this trespass. It was trespass," she insists, "but it was necessary to become who we are!"

At this point in the tale, he began to see the story of Adam and Eve as a primary evolutionary tale, more about natural history than actual biblical history.

"Men and women then decided that some of the family should split off—with a few settling in Central Asia and others in what became known as Europa."

"This must have been a painful set of decisions," Varlissima adds. "Perhaps this was caused more by catastrophe than rational decision," he says, pulling her head closer to his.

The record does not yet fully explain this. There is a long pause for a dream interruption. Scientists scramble in the dream without answers. While a few others proceeded, most settled in Asia and Europe. How could this even have happened? When you study the rigor of the fossil record, it is nothing short of magical, this dispersion of man.

Then the most astonishing part of the tale began . . .

"The fossil record now claims that perhaps as few as five men and a dozen women, this small extended family cluster,

walked across the Bering Strait into a new world of corn and sun and canyons." This dream was multi-layered. It allowed them both to feel certain, as a shiver was sent up their spines, that Varlissima and Colette would have been among these original women of trespass, preparing the new warriors.

It did not matter if he made that grade. He was blessed by having the thought about the key role of these women. What mattered was that Colette and Varlissima were there, with him now, capable of bringing new life into the mix of his mind, despite its harsh climate. This is the long view of the journey, the journey where survival itself is the surprise.

Races mix, eons pass, many go missing; in the end, some continue and survive. After so much pleasure, there was even more room for trespass. After this elaborate dream, what mattered was to step behind social sophistication—and to keep walking, as a species—in order to descend deeper than the presumed supremacy of the rational. This is what he thought about in that African mask in his front office.

His African mask was as bold as a Greek myth, full of these complex imperatives on how to live. It gave him a license to accept his aging, to no longer feel the need to hold the entire family upon his shoulders. *Succession was beginning to matter as much as self-definition.* This mask became a product of ultimate realism, showing him a world full of evil, unpredictable storms, rising waters, difficult friendships, dignity incarnate, and inevitable death and defeat. In contrast to this mask, it was modern religion that had become unrealistic, with its expectations of certain and earned salvation, and its simplification of wrong.

This mask helped him describe his mortal life as it really was—that is, fragile, threatened, uncertain, never consistently happy, and full of surprise. The three of them forged ahead, survivors—Colette, Varlissima, Bruce.

MEETING DARLENE

There was nothing intellectual, nothing sexual, in the appearance of Darlene in their lives. Everyone in his life who met Darlene—lawyers, bankers, alliance partners, friends—felt her magic in different ways. She never finished college, but she gave advanced lessons to many.

Things had come full circle, in a sense. In youth, we are allowed to surround ourselves with stimulating folks from teammates to early lovers. But as we age, these people become dramatically more constrained by the conventions of marriage and family.

But occasionally, something magical and different happens.

Darlene was liked by Varlissima and Colette.

They enjoyed her. They trusted her.

Darlene, they knew, was special to him in a primal way. In a parallel universe, Jay was important to him for inspiration. It was Darlene who jump-started new business ventures in his team and in him. She was a secret weapon without any arrows or slings. At times, she would prove essential to his family. She knew something about his soul. She knew a great deal about his family and his history. She was a great listener who paid attention. She knew how to protect the pride. Slovak families often had special ladies hang around like this in the deeper past.

He had a strong ego that repelled criticism, but she had a new way to enter and twist his inner self. He often wrote his best stuff, his most creative passages, after a short whimsical exchange with her.

She always came up with zingers that he'd find surprising and fun to think through. Once, after spending three hours filing literary and corporate documents with him in the back office, she suddenly said, "Do not corner me, Bruce."

He began to think through the moment of sudden rightness when he decided to let her into his inner circle, not just as a friend, not just as a worker, but as a soul helping to manage the inner sanctum of his ever-widening circle of friends and colleagues. Rasputin might have been a man turned female to come back as Darlene No, he cautioned, it wasn't like that, she had no interest in any grab for power. She was just having fun.

He often wanted Darlene's secret assessment of a deal—even if he already had a few lawyers and key proven consultants in on the talks. She always saw something they had collectively missed about the essence of the visitors.

They sealed their deal while going to a fundraiser at Fort Ticonderoga. The year was 2012. Colette wasn't yet sixteen. There they sat, in the same place where 400 years before, Samuel de Champlain and the Huron fathers had signed their peace agreement, which lasted through the Revolutionary War. They agreed on the ride back to Saratoga that "they would work together for life, as they and their families aged." A very strange pact indeed. In the process, Colette came to understand how her father needed muses, not mistresses.

He now had three outstanding women in his life.

REVENUE FROM
MANY PLACES

His management firm now had complex teams working on food security in Africa for Walmart, ASDA and others. He had several larger contracts with Merck, the pharma giant, on carbon neutrality, where he worked a team of world trends experts, several investment CEOs and doctors, a total of eight experts across four years. He began to serve the global firms like bp of London that brought oil and gas to a world of 7 billion souls in their transformation. He continued to run twice a year his high-end, multi-year benchmarking workshop on innovation, carbon threats, and energy trends, including at any given workshop at least fifteen of the largest firms in the world. CEOs, board members, company founders, investors, paid to enroll.

He was not slowing down, merely increasing his reach and impact on the firm, which for a few decades took on this global reach. It, as if organic, brought revenue from many places. He also needed less time in the office, as his back office was mighty and strong, and again run by women more organized and more deliberate than he could ever prove to be. Marti Simmons was with him for a decade, perhaps the best decade, as she was accountant, organizer, and great with the teams. He began to feel that these women spoke with many tongues, and that their differences made his personal competitiveness and the male senior earners more sensible.

Yet the larger his practice became, the more he found comfort in smaller, distinct, non-intellectual items, such as that statue of the deer whose antlers could hold candles. He would come to call this "the Darlene Effect." Perhaps this was the ultimate end zone of training he got from a lifetime of reading the classics, folks like his super heroes Walt Whitman, George Orwell, and Winston Churchill. Each day when he wrote, he'd spend some time with those heroes before making any business deals or checks. He was less and less a money maker and more a shaper of alliances. This technique of partnering with much larger organizations like Globe Scan or Standard & Poor's or Calvert offered his efforts more social impact. He had become a person capable of articulating partnerships and alliances that helped several parties grow at once.

He had placed this bronze artifact on the fireplace mantel in honor of the poet Wallace Stevens, who had written "Anecdote of the Jar," one of his favorite simple poems. Like the deer in his office, that jar, which had been placed upon a hill in Tennessee, held dominion over everything. He felt his deer a fine and appropriate substitute for Darlene's good cheer, as Darlene would remarry and move South. He kept her spirit and attitude in the deer. It was all odd, and wonderful like a totem.

A treasure trove surrounded this deer, adding grandeur to his ever-mounting collection of books. He loved reading regional history now, however detailed, between business calls. He would reread books like *Bloody Mohawk: The French and Indian War & American Revolution*. He lived in the past, as he won the future. He was both past mistakes and future solutions. He felt Whitmanesque, Churchillian. And still Bruce.

It all clicked one day. He had bought the Bentley estate, which had been built around 1760, to bring it into his family's future. He thought about its succession of owners—the seven generations of Bentleys—the way they gathered the fieldstones to build the church across the road in 1824, the way Doctor Hunt bought it from the Bentleys during the Great Depression, and in extending it, readied it for his purchase.

The entire history clicked one day. He must stop roaming the world. He more actively became the investor in his homestead and in a range of stocks. He must make his writing and his home matter. He could feel succession now in his bones. He cultivated the feeling more and more by doing less and less. Money came around. It settled near him like the magic in the deer's antlers.

CURIOUS LIKE
A CATAPULT

Words were his weapons, ever since he was a kid. Yet as his wealth compounded, and as he kept asking his mother's question, "What is enough?" he felt curious and motivated. He felt serious harm to his certainty when he could not hear his own words in the foreign editions of his books. Hearing himself in Italian felt almost good, but Korean and Portuguese felt odd.

He wondered, turning even older, about the boy still in his "propulsiveness."

This was an endlessly young word used by his friend and life-long contractor Frank Weaver.

At first Frank said, "I thought the founder was impulsive, always striving. But over time I saw he was more like a little Steve Jobs, without the need of many machines. Bruce's continuous impact on a range of people was not impulsiveness. It was propulsiveness."

He liked the word "propulsiveness" enough to adopt it for the last third of his life. It made him curious enough to create a foundation for writers under forty; for other reasons, he started getting lucrative corporate Board appointments. He found he was still a boy at all this, curious like a catapult. Even his Wikipedia page began to mimic how this propulsion shaped his life.

He began to ask: is native propulsion the same as longing and joy? Is it any different from the joy his daughter feels when her cat sits on her lap? Is it, this longing, exactly like the octane of his youth we find in everyone on the court's engine? Basketball was the great leveling bounce of his youth, while words kept making him curious and even warlike. It was the readers and their feedback that helped him decide he lived a writer's life.

According to our male-dominant culture, catapults have captivated boys longer than rubber. We saw it in the tall tales of David, smashing Goliath in his broad stupid forehead with any stone, a stone nearby. Boys do not need to strategize very much to prove brutal and effective.

He remembered shooting paper cups off the head of a willing neighbor boy when he was ten, with a Christmas gifted bow and arrow. It was not much fun. But it became doable when others gathered around. The key was to have others in tow, in a secret boy society, like when he saw his uncle's cat delight in cornering a mouse.

Before Goliath, boys used biblical leather for their slingshots, not Walmart mimics, and he now asked: So what did the girls finger when the boys were shooting cups off of each other's heads? Freud naively asked, What do women want? When in fact we all frolic in youth, and we all know life is short.

The wind changes as it alters memory, gender, culture, style. You would be a fool to expect certainty in any community, as so much happened on the side, between the catapults and arrows. Big Bad Bruce, it was a children's story that never quite quit. Equipped with very little except what we all have, he knew, as a native, never to simply watch. Propulsive.

To push past the severe cliffs and daily barriers of ordinary life, he started to zig and to zag and then to zig again, as he gave up the stern logic of lyric and accepted that springtime matters more than genre or the elements of style.

This shift, this maturing, did not happen overnight. One day he simply did not stop and put the catapult and the arrows in the attic. Instead, this subtle shift helped him understand the brilliant books of Annie Dillard and Edna O'Brien. It was simple arrogance for him to conclude he had advanced to an understanding of the female brain by marriage or by the birth of Colette. Annie Dillard writes in her memoir:

A writer's childhood may well have been the occasion of his only firsthand experience. Writers read literary biography, and surround themselves with other writers; deliberately to enforce in themselves the ludicrous notion that living in a single room with plenty of pieces of paper is enough.

He called his small room in a large home his daily descent into a miner's cave. He'd pick up his pickaxe and start swinging each morning in the dark cave. He did not know when he was near the gold seam above his head in the rock; all he knew was the athletic value in swinging each day. Annie Dillard is fun to read but is also annoying to read. She fails to note that when you re-emerge from the cave, from that little room of the writer's rumination, friends and lovers note the gold dust in your eyebrows.

Born curious, he was destined to keep the boy in him, to catapult his cares and his words beyond simple blame. This was both irritating and a cause for his thanks. At times he felt the oceans too large, and the land too limitless.

CHOOSING
THE RIGHT POND

One of the best books he'd never read was *Choosing the Right Pond*, by Robert Frank, a professor of economics at Cornell. He brought this book at least a dozen times on his Caneel Bay vacations in the Virgin Islands, but never found the time to read it. Manta rays and schools of fish were what filled those days. He would mail the book to Room 13 at this former Rockefeller resort, but never opened it. By the tenth visit, he just mailed it out of ritual.

He read much into that title. This concept of choosing the right pond helped him escape some of the remorse that surrounded him during the first half of his middle age, and through most of the depression he felt in youth. How could that happen? Well, it allowed him to become more social and far less internal. It was about the right pond, not him. It was about business, and the business of books, nothing more. It was wrong to think too much about the vastness of the ocean. Freedom was about choosing the right size for his options. After choosing Saratoga as his pond, he found himself standing alone in his yard one day and thinking, *"How perfectly silly it is to discount the wondrous."*

He kept an image of Caneel Bay, with two boats and a dock, in his mind even in winter when at home. This new-found ability to ignore the experts, to forget about the return in the equation, to sidestep complexity that will not yield, offered a kind of protection that was deeper than his middle-aged remorse. He was, in a sense, becoming priceless.

After many a business trip or speaking engagement, he would sit near the pond across from the Old Stone Church, chomping on a Churchill cigar and eyeing his blooming flowerbeds. He really hated TV, really liked radio, but liked the interaction of large groups even more. Sometimes Darlene or Varlissima or Colette would join him during these peaceful garden visits. This family bliss was beyond his normal fears of middle age.

He came to recognize a set of higher facts that he wanted to pass along to future generations: "Hey youth! Watch out! You can piss away your youth trying to decide which ocean to jump into and when. But you can become quite anxious at the beach, doing nothing. You must choose the right pond."

He saw that in choosing the *right* pond, he had entered the near-perfect future. He described this state to Varlissima one night, and she said: "You always get this way when finishing a book."

"What way?" he asked. "All warm and fuzzy and mystical." He felt as if he had broken a code that mattered now, since he brought those same feelings away from book writing into his life. It was in the tone of things now—in the wind by his home, not the leaves whirling in the wind. The atmosphere at the Old Stone Church felt like a crossing.

Then one day everything changed again.

He calculated the anticipated values of his eight TIAA-CREF retirement accounts, tabulated the worth of his firm if projected with modesty, added the value of his home and its related and unrelated property, and decided, "Shit, I can become a pensioner." And he did.

To celebrate the decision, Varlissima planned a surprise trip to the beaches on Long Island where he was born. He felt at last that he understood the power in a compassionate Buddha.

A MOTHER'S DEATH

He had always loved his mother, but now that she was missing, he found that he loved the remaining women in his life even more.

And this is precisely why it made the ordinary elements in his life extraordinary. It seemed odd, but the more time he invested with these women, the greater the impact and profit of his work teams. He wondered why it took three decades for him to discover this about team success.

He attributed his good luck to how he had been raised by his mother. Once he had learned how best to invest in memory, the death of his mother extended his wings in a manner larger than common sense.

He came to believe that, as promised, Lillian was keeping it all tied together up there for them—so they would not, could not, fail. She had given him the logic of remorse. The logic of remorse is hard to explain, especially to men, but it proves priceless in its consequences. Remorse proves liberating. He could say to his lover, "I must get to work. Sorry, but I miss you already." He could say to a business partner, "Sorry, I must leave for vacation—my daughter is waiting, but I miss you already." He'd say to himself, *"I have bigger things before me."*

Scot Paltrow, his Cornell undergraduate roommate, and a journalist of renown for Reuters after the *Wall Street Journal*, said to him upon the death of his mother: "Hey Bruce I remember you chomping down her food, as you read Freud's *Interpretation of Dreams* during your freshman year. So presumptuous! Polish sausage with Freudian ambitions! Now after her passing, I think you should write *The Interpretation of Teams*, with this odd preoccupation you have with CEOs."

He wrote that book as *Doing More with Teams*, a sequel for Wiley to his bestseller. It did not take away his sense of pain in losing his mother, in becoming an orphan. Although the frequency of his calls with his biological sister Terry in Florida and Georgia increased dramatically over time, he was not able to escape the weight of that loss.

Yet still, he had bigger things before him, despite the loss.

Miraculously, he had to admit he had become one of the lucky ones.

A FATHER'S DEATH

He would never finish this thought path because he had so little to go on. For decades, he had blamed everyone he knew for his father's death. Having been raised by his grandmother, mother, and sister, he had to invent his masculinity—from muscle and bone to making his place in a world of markets.

His father would break his long silence only on rare occasions. In this way, Walter was the opposite of his mother, who could return on a dime. He found this not sad, but odd.

In his World War II pictures, Walter was tall, thin, and quiet looking, and he also looked reserved—not meant to be in this world very long. Walter had never really spoken to him as a parent, so Bruce had no real direct recollection of the sound of his father's voice, or the look on his face when he held him as a child—so all of this needed, wanted, to be reconstructed by the higher winds of memory.

In one faded photo, Walt—with cigarette in hand, hanging around a rock in Hawaii during his days serving in the Pacific—looked much like Eric Arthur Blair, before he became known to the world as George Orwell.

He had been Walter's child for such a short time—less than three years, two months, and a few long summer days. Yet Walt returned to him on occasion, especially when he was under stress. He came to an important conclusion: In a writer's life, where rumination runs like a fear through many years, it pays to recall the details and death of your father and mother.

This calculation of fatherly loss—like Freud standing before his father burning in dream—matters. This kind of loss is as useful as prayer.

WE FLOWER
UNDER STRESS

In the middle of the night, he had one of his feverish thought paths. He was edging sixty. He knew that many modern men either retired or died within a decade or two of that signal age. He had already consumed a half-century and more in finding his place. His father had left at thirty-nine, and he had cousins who checked out in their forties. This mathematical urgency began to run beside his days.

He would write more and spend less time on business. Again and again he'd streamline his staff, eliminating with some pain those he loved but no longer needed to succeed.

This led to his next big thought in reshuffling his life: he should not stop, as he always flowered under stress. He sought stress. Without it, he might cease. The next night's dream was intense. He felt the dream in the third person, as if his mother was lecturing him about the actions he was taking, but at the same time, understanding those actions for the first time . . .

> *You are with Sally in her basement; her mother's washing machine is making noise above the groans, as her father, who is also the school principal, is cutting the lawn.*
>
> *You can see him from the basement window mowing lane by lane, moving farther away from you as you stand against the wall with the tight body of Sally nearby. You experience the stress. You press her groin against that wall, and rub, and she wants that, knowing that in minutes her father will be too far away from the basement wall to be able to look in easily at two fifteen-year olds.*
>
> *But as long as her father's angle of receding takes him away from the angle of seeing you, she wants more.*
>
> *As the stress mounts, you know he can bend over at any second into discovery, and you know he will come back near you and peer in soon enough. At the same time, you can feel the moisture in her pants, and you know that you will always—somehow—flower under stress.*
>
> *This is the stress of success.*
>
> *Like big Dutch tulip bulbs, we pop up from the earth in the shadow of our parents, and while they give us the food and shelter of early growth, they also help us flower by leaving.*

Life is simply too large, too lusty, too loving to stop this pursuit of stress and joy, profit and pleasure. The dream ends . . . To try to make sense of it, he recalls a passage from Walt Whitman's *Leaves of Grass* in which he notes:

> *Youth, large, lusty, loving—*
> *youth full of grace, force, fascination.*
> *Do you know that Old Age may come after you*
> *with equal grace, force, fascination?*

He had loved that passage throughout his life.

So often, an experience in his life had come full circle. What started as a nightmare, a fear, had become a poetic lesson, a vignette of memory that recites an essence, a meaning, and a hope.

TORN BY THE CONCERNS

By now, many were asking how did a poor "almost immigrant" boy make and save millions? How had he roamed so far from Long Island, then roamed into so many distinct multinationals? Those questions arose suddenly in his soul.

He loved the questions faced by the press after each book; he felt good about the attention.

Like a tear in his knees, this became a common daily part of his compositional history, the way he was propelled to write.

Could he answer with the same boldness about the thousands of business leaders he had met to make himself? Or was there something particularly perverse about that thought? He was frankly torn by these questions, yet they kept coming at him, and each new book he published only increased their rate of attack.

This was a part of his eccentric good luck: people turned to him to help him, and he accepted the attention. He attributed his knowledge of teamwork to all his years as a street basketball player. And perhaps the maturing of his organizations could be attributed to this higher fact: he strove in everything he did to remain coachable. There was always a way to improve, to be taught a new move, so many hung near to give him advice, most of which he found a way to use, thankfully.

What drew him to business was the complexity, the energy of it, the relationships.

Across three decades, his guests enjoyed fun and cheer and learning at the same time, and paid big bucks for the chance. He imagined these workshops vividly beforehand, planning them to a T with his staff, and he came to think that there was something classic in assembling them. It was not so much a party of leaders as a team of leaders, and not so much a gathering across many regions as a sanctuary he had made.

He failed several times across his fifties and sixties to train deputies that could replace him in his leadership workshops. Those skills combined a strange kind of microaggression to get to the bottom of groups, and teams. And he tried to find his replacement in Greece with Michael Spanos, and failed, and then with several of his past students, each of which inflated their value with lessening results.

Okay, he was one of the lucky ones. Success was not about self-help, after all. It was about helping many others: gradually, a reputation for helping many rose around him and his teams.

The life of business proved to be fun. He did not need to revise his business plans. It all resided in the magic of relationships based on aligning money, people and rules. He should revise his books, not his business plan. That discovery itself proved worth millions more.

Yet it was the joy in writing that questioned all this earning. He would let the company and the group shrink before he let someone else take it in the wrong direction. He knew this to be a founder's folly, yet it stuck with him after all his failures to find a deputy that could take over.

ALL ICE IS DANGEROUS

Of course, success does not isolate you from danger or fear. The more you write about it the more you need to write.

He had a nightmare of a frozen river, the Racquette, near the apartment Varlissima and he shared during their days working for Clarkson. It was a nightmare that travelled with him to Saratoga and Istanbul and almost each time he slept in London.

Close to midnight one winter night, he had seen a bike rider circling on the frozen Raquette River in Potsdam, New York. During the frigid winters, the surface of the Raquette, which courses through the town, would freeze and remain solid for several months.

This long-distant memory froze in his mind for decades. He could not outpace it, for it was connected

with a tragedy. That same winter, a fellow Clarkson professor—one with whom he and Varlissima had shared a
rented triplex—had died beneath that same ice in a terrible accident. It was a devastating event that left his col-
league's young children without a father. Being fatherless
himself, Bruce felt a painful connection with the tragedy
on many levels.

The haunting image of this lone bike rider was both good
and bad, both liberating and utterly depressing. This
faceless person, who rode in circles on the frozen river,
had shown him that life could remain magically open for
trying most anything, while others sank beneath the ice.
He realized he had become like that bike rider: skidding
on the ice of business, riding with joy into the literary.
And again, like the night rider, he recognized his balance was mostly luck, as others fell beneath the same ice.
People thought of him as a decent professor at Clarkson.
He thought of himself as a writer and businessman. It was
this shifting set of differences that wore thin with time,
so he had to move to survive. His success wasn't based
at all on courage, but simply on the art of remaining
balanced and open, like the survivor on the ice.

Much of his life had become a balancing act to stay
erect as he bumped into things and people each day. This
balancing took the daily disciplines he knew from his
basketball days. He took many spins, tried many teams,
ran after many gigs. He was no professor in retrospect.
He was a boy, curious in action. He wrote a motto to act
by: "Actors speak of imaginary things as if they are real.
Academics speak of real things as if they are imaginary."

Yes, all ice remained dangerous.

All ice is dangerous, but that is what gave his life its beauty and its stark brilliance. What enabled his survival remained a mystery.

VENTURE
UNDERSTANDING

He found visualizing the near future a useful weapon. It helped him mature and sift through what really mattered. He could now dismiss most requests almost instantly; for example, he never financed extensive risk evaluations, nor did he pay much for legal advice. Instead, he executed fast on what mattered most.

He began to look at dangers in business. It was wonderful to be able to analyze and think through risks. It reminded him often of pivots, of moves on the basketball court from his youth. Danger was beautiful to him. It was several lovely young women inviting him into the lily pond next door. While the decision to terminate staff was never easy, and he lost sleep over each decision, he found it neither sad nor puzzling when necessary. His venture understanding, his embrace of the venture itself, always prevailed.

He thought of the market in which he worked as a pond. Survival in that pond, where it was easy to drown, was about the teams, not about the terms. It was about the pond, not the profit. It was never about him.

That is what he loved the most about business.

He was often the one to jump into the pond first and take its temperature before others would harvest the lilies. For him, it was all about preparing for the muddy moments when the road gets dark—so, if necessary, he could throw the spark. He judged his team by secret measures like trust. This wasn't so much talent collection, as talent liberation. The most alert in his staff like Gordon Lambert of Calgary and Ken Strassner of Atlanta, executive leaders in their own days at major firms, understood him to be about ventures. But many in the group did not, and he had a few very ugly firings after he reached a certain age. He no longer wanted to be a babysitter of staff, but instead work with high octane allies and their staff.

He did his time with discipline—always asking himself before diving in, "What can we get done, and what must we leave undone?" This made him pursue a select life. Most in business called this an exit strategy. He considered it always an entrance strategy, a channel to something more magical and more mysterious, namely relationships and friendships, agreements in action.

DINNER WITH SALMAN RUSHDIE

Less than a year before a crazy zealot stabbed the great writer in his throat and chest and eye, Salman Rushdie dined with Paul Grondahl and William Kennedy. He balanced a small table at the New York State Writers Institute in Albany. The conversation was a feast, full of word play and insight.

He had entertained three sets of audiences that day, with grace and force, a graduate group of literary scholars in waiting, a large mixed public lecture and platform, and a smaller set of fellow writers—and now Salman was relaxing.

His mind was as clear as Adirondack Mountain spring melt. Crystal cool, at times, so alert it proved chilling. He spoke with him about Herman Melville. He was generous, peppering me with memories of the semester I spent studying everything Melville wrote during graduate school.

That night Salman cited passages from Melville's *Typee* and *Omoo*, his first books, then rapidly picked at how *Moby Dick* had to come about after these masterful early travel books. Salman had these books ready in his mind as if he had read each of them the day before. We covered a range of writers this way, from Jay Parini to other contemporaries. He carried their phrasing and purposes with him like friends.

Salman Rushdie said: "The moment you decide a set of ideas to be immune from artful criticism, satire, public derision or splendid contempt, real freedom of thought becomes over-salted and compressed." He sipped some wine I poured. He laughed openly often. Our great host, the Executive Director Paul Grondahl, was so gracious, as was Kennedy, now in his nineties.

He was afraid to say anything about his mixing of the meal with the literature, but I created in my notebook that next morning a new word for his frenzy and for Salman Rushdie's special speed of mind: jumbogumbo. He was fun to be with, but more than amusing. How cruel life can be that such a master is struck by a knife.

8 APRIL 2012

Across any lonely highway sits a church open in the spring. It is Easter, April 8, 2012. His book *Doing More with Less* has been a bestseller on a couple of lists since its release in March. In thanks, he went to service.

Up until then, some had thought him an ordinary business writer, yet he had always insisted that he wrote about business and society. This style that jumped best for him was personal narrative, where a book like *Doing More with Less* was part memoir, part revelation, part social history. As this short book crossed over that spring, he felt new growth like a few wildflowers in a very organized British garden. He felt this short cross over book was best understood as a modernization and popularization of Freud, Darwin, and Marx in the guise of Ben Franklin.

Many read in English but only a few read from the UK. The American and Canadian and Australian markets proved huge. In joy, he listened to the Easter ceremony, and wondered, without the walking and the music in the opening procession, do we lose joy in ceremony?

From the dead of winter, the soul of the soil does arise, claims Psalm 139. Hallelujah, expels Leonard Cohen, with his seductively broken popular wings, chained to his lover's chair, like Sampson a few haircuts before Easter.

Grant us life without serious harm. Cleanse us dear spring, from the evils within. Forget any appeal in fame or recognition. Each reader, he noted, has many musical keys before them. The parish staff promises a secular egg hunt for the children of the community, with eggs colored in a fashion friendlier than Putin.

From top to bottom, his faith is as boiled down now as an egg, like the dome of an Italian cathedral in Florence. He will have many books in him; he likes the feeling, the ceremony. The tulips in his yard, and in the church garden, have risen from their tomb, and rejoice in a hope he knew longer in its eternal glory than his personal ambitions.

Humility is the hymn that allows invention, a new text, and new reason to try, as birds pop worms from the maples, and without goat or donkey near, we can visualize an ancient reentry to community after this service in full. Was it that his mother's faith made him a man in full? Or was it that first meeting with Varlissima, when with crutch in hand, she noted that "mobility is a gift"? Or perhaps this all came to a head when Tom Wolfe, after his bestseller, wrote to him in a nice letter, "come on down to join The Lotos Club, and dine with me."

The lesson is that winter will put us again to death by nailing our mobility on a tree. While only the imagination is free, the fee is time. On the third day of February count on black ice to be back, and no intelligent birds in the sky.

This is the liturgy of spring, as the people sit and read. Spring shall not die but live, it is suggested during the collection, where Paul claims he worked harder than others in working the legend.

Thinking through his good fortunes with Varlissima, Tom Wolfe, his books, he became more humble rather than less. The themes of the poor, and the suffering of the many, and the two angels the church sees in the absent Christ are about mercy and giving. Early in this first week of April, while it is still dark, a writer strives to make sense of what has happened in a visible way to his work and his life.

The weather has become severe; the sick, and the weak, and the dying are part and parcel of each spring now. Glory to the spring, in joy and hope, let it begin again. Glory to the new roads now available to him and his family. His Creative Force Foundation would carry on through many springs.

THE ELEPHANT QUEEN

One night he dreamt about an elephant queen, who in a rather nasal way, hooted, "Bruce, remember to inform, persuade, and delight." She carried, in this dream, all Freudian and Darwinian traditions in her gait, swaying her pure white tusks and heavy legs.

She used her nose to milk some cows across from the Stone Church in this dream, which haven't been there for the last hundred years. Cows only roamed the Stone Church neighborhood, like the slaves, when the place was a regional farm for the minister's family. But here in the dream, the Devon cows awaited her attention, as did three pregnant wolves representing my favorite cities of Lucca, Belfast, and Athens near the bay.

The Elephant Queen did not need a last name like Madonna or Lady Gaga. She used her tusks to probe precision out of me, both in my prose and in my face. Her steps stampeded the crowds into alertness, as she was herself the contest and the conquest, the hope and the fulfillment.

When one creative soul pays tribute to several leaders—like in this dream I had of Freud, Darwin, and Marx in a single supper—you create a community of trust. You need to acknowledge the queen, but you must also be seen by the greats, those writers who shaped your soul.

Civilization has its discontents. Retirement has its discontents. Everyday has its discounts from joy. Yet the Elephant Queen reminds one in dream that self-awareness is possible if we inform, persuade and delight.

SACRED MEMORY

People do not need to understand water in order to jump deeply into it. It is the same with the vastness of memory. The deeper you jump into what you do not understand about it, the more you feel what is sacred in memory. He learned that by rereading Freud's *Interpretation of Dreams*, and Darwin's *Origin of Species*.

If he thought hard enough about his international trips, he could sense—and then worship—the wind behind the many close calls he had experienced. These memories, as he aged, became more sacred and certain than even his favorite first hundred books.

It was simply marvelous to have survived so long on the road, an idler in more than a third of the world's mega-cities. This provided three new thoughts. First, his memory itself was becoming sacred, in the most appreciative way. Second, he felt at times in God's corner—that is, he felt advantaged by fate. Finally, he was becoming the type of lucky fool who would giggle at his own funeral—for if death came by, he had already gotten away with so much that he would not feel cheated, like his father.

When he saw Colette, Varlissima, and Darlene in the same day, he felt "this is the only heaven I'll ever be invited to."

At seventy-six, it was no longer worthwhile to even count the number of places he had visited. There simply were too many to matter, or to fully recall. Since his late fifties, he did choose to go on tours of Australia, Turkey, and Ireland simply because he had never been there before. Yet now, he returned to many cities simply because he had let forty years slip by since he had last visited.

He had last walked the miracle mile that descended from Edinburgh Castle, with its crystal palace and historic prison dungeons, when he was a student of Shakespeare. But now, at seventy-six, he returned to give a series of lectures on life and the business of life, and to dine with the leaders of the region. He was the same man, with the same sensibility, but now the stage had grown tremendously, and mysteriously. These returns beckoned a misty feeling in him, of high emotion, where youthful facts of sensual recollection were blended now with new sacred memories.

These recollections connected to places made him more human—so human an animal. Many recall, in later life, that when Pandora's box of travel is unhinged and then opened, the world slips out in a fashion both endless and vastly open. This now caused elation and exhaustion in the old man. There is seldom anything like a diet on the road; a whiskey diet is perhaps the closest he ever achieved consistently while traveling. Yet the great myths of old informed him about the risks he had survived, without the risk of too much whiskey. These myths of Pandora and the Midas touch helped him. He came to accept the risks inherent in the tales of Pandora without allowing his innocence to be compromised by them. Things pop out in travel that you must reconcile, or else cease to be human.

Memory was sacred in a shared universal way now, but it was also his own, vastly personal.

What remained of those memories was sacred, easily discernible if associated with images of the people along the way—the taxi driver who'd warned him off a bad neighborhood; the good friend he'd never seen again who had told him which dives to avoid and which places could be enjoyed safely; the foreign police who had helped him even without speaking his language or understanding the nature of his need. Diplomacy while traveling can be tricky, like doing fast field work with a chainsaw. But somehow, he always survived.

On one trip, after leaving northern Greece with his translator, they were met near Istanbul by men with machine guns, visibly hating him, but waving him on because he looked like a powerful American businessman. The same thing happened to him while traveling between the Turkish and Greek borders. To have survived Istanbul, Tokyo, Belfast, Melbourne, Manhattan, Paris, Rome, Canton, Sydney, Athens, Houston, Calgary, and the guns of Detroit so many times, was to feel the hand of God swing past. He wrote about this in *Carpe Articulum*, an international arts journal, where he wrote for Hadassah Broscova, a Russian-American-Scottish editor of some real flamboyance, in a short piece called "An Idler in the City." It was that piece that got him hired by bp for his knowledge of trends in megacities.

Each city had a marvelously different feel, an inherent personality; some were warm and exciting, others rude, troubling, and suffocating—like those Thanksgiving relatives you know too well, who cannot travel out of their ruts of idle superiority and judgment. All of these great cities, so vividly compacted and different from the beach where he was born, shared some common traits in his memory. They were dense, lively, and the answer to climate impacts over time. If we could rebuild the infrastructure, he argued with giant firms like Jacobs Engineering and Lockheed Martin, then we can solve more than half of the greenhouse problems by 2035.

No matter how dismal, dirty, or congested, the cities were growing on Earth: people were surviving in great hordes, and this alone made him feel embarrassed when he arrived depressed. He would shed that skin like a snake, when he saw how poor and how miserable many remained. This helped him escape the worst of his American feelings. "How dare I weigh myself down when they have so much less?" he thought again and again, until he felt free of a weight around his neck.

This was a strange and effective kind of medicine. He was one of the lucky ones, one of those articulate few who can surround themselves with risk and find the rewards in it. People—not just his friends—now called him an optimist.

HIS SECOND
OBSESSION

If reading classics, and worrying about climate change were his first obsessions, the second obsession, like the first, had a reflective quality. He was always aware of always performing. This made every conversation he found himself in a performance—where jobs derived from a random airport flight, and staffers arrived from very funny and public exchanges that proved of great consequence. He was on, they said, all day long.

He once hired one of his most profitable young staffers after spotting her on a bicycle outside his post office. Just like that, he decided to walk over to this stranger and start a conversation, telling her about the CEO he had just called. She was impressed, moved to his town, and doubled in value to the firm each year for the six years before she left for Goldman Sachs. She had no initial expertise in his field, but he was certain in an instant she'd work out simply from that initial conversation outside the post office. He did this "risk hiring" again and again as his firm grew. Sometimes it was a disaster, most of the time it worked. There was no need for technical expertise; he could train that.

He guessed he glued onto this behavior first on the basketball court, where the great scouts were hidden in all audiences. You must be sportive in your seriousness. Born with a love of reading, he cultivated a certain forcefulness in business settings, a penchant for leaning into his future with wit, a boy on the loose. Work had to be fun, as well as fundamental.

He never was high enough in the organizations he advised to lose his head when failure surrounded his clients. He often felt like a jester at court, who could be ignored during the rush for accountability.

Varlissima didn't need to know the details, another beauty in having a smart Sicilian as a lifelong wife. She had no patience for the complexities of currencies, earnings, and taxes overseas. But he showed Colette the paper notes with a kind of fatherly glee.

Here was the queen who graced the front of the Canadian dollar, her expression happier and less stern than the image on the British pound. Here was the South African twenty-rand note, with a smiling Nelson Mandela on one side, elephants emerging from the other, and prehistoric hunters pursuing gazelles on the security screen. Here were the crisp notes from his clients around the world. He now kept them in small boxes to view and share.

In a sense, liberating the creative rather than the professional side of himself allowed him to change the work-play balance. Relationships, respect, and then revenue: the mantra defined his life work when he was not writing.

When writing, all fell away into being near fear and joy.

VISITING BELFAST, IRELAND

He was now a bestseller, with a speaking agent who sold him for kicks to Ireland, Scotland, Istanbul, Japan, Australia, and in between. This caused further pain, fear, and joy. In visiting Belfast, that most industrialized and troubled place of superb and friendly people, it began to make some more ancient sense.

Patricia loved Americans. During the troubles she escorted Senator George Mitchell on early visits to Belfast.

When he met Patricia before his days with her at Queen's University, she listened intently with an Irish jingle and smile. He recited a few stanzas to her of the great songs of Van Morrison. She finished the stanzas.

"Oh he is a bad boy," she noted, "but we all love him. He moves around town in a hoodie, arriving in our events as the audience is seated. We love him dear."

She toured me around two days before my talk on "doing more with less." In relaxed clothing, we toured with a string of guests through the celebrated Clinton rooms, commemorating the Mitchell-Clinton accords. Patricia did her homework, noting to the resident Director that he too had served the first term of the Clinton White House.

In his visits to Dublin and elsewhere in Ireland they always woke to fine stories when he told them he was a writer. From coast to Trinity to the Technical schools, lively dialogue filled the days. It is a place for American-based writers.

What remained lovely and lasting in his memories of Patricia and Belfast was the sense of narrative joy in the cadence of her hosting—"let us wander, these short hours, a few of my favorite churches where you may wish to buy your mom or wife a gift." She later brought him a signed copy of Van Morrison lyrics.

Patricia delivered over three hundred to his late afternoon talk and kept a joyful correspondence through the years.

Belfast, oh sweet Belfast, your troubles are complex. And yet your love of language—its cadence and tilt—bring life to your docks, schools, and song-full streets. Each time he hears his songs in Walmart or the supermarket, he meets Van Morrison again.

STIRLING IS STIRRING, SCOTLAND

Here in Scotland, on a book tour, he enjoyed meeting the colorful dinner guests, talkative and supportive. The Chancellor of Stirling College, well-set with a metallic vest of centuries of pins and emblems, greeted his full table of guests—at least twenty—exclaiming:

"Oh, Dr. Piasecki, may I call you Bruce? I see you are a good enough chap. You enjoy our new Sports complex before coming to this dinner; I saw you talking up the faculty over tea. Do you mind if I take off this damn ceremonial jacket vest? It weighs down my dinner! It has been weighing me down, us Chancellors, since about 1540."

He spoke not far from where, in 1297, William Wallace defeated the English forces at Stirling Bridge, made famous again for our generation by Mel Gibson in the film *Braveheart*. But like the Chancellor, this was a jacket they wore, this history, each day. The woman faculty linguist, who followed him to the dinner from the gym offering an amplitude of advice on other things to do while there in Stirling, noted that the original Anglo Saxon word for Stirling means "place of strife."

How appropriate, he felt, staring down the Chancellor, full of tale and joy, as the visiting American stood out from the scene like a basketball giant hobbling up the steep stone steps of Stirling Castle. Campus was friendly.

Oh, bloody Scotland, where highland hikers take in the grand spreading sky near Loch Tulla, you can almost forget cars for a day even in this century.

In memory, it was a grand four-hour dinner conversation. The faculty came from places he hoped to visit, Angus and Dundee, Perth and Grampian.

While he would return within a decade with wife and daughter, and then again many other times for business in Edinburgh or Glasgow, he never made it quite like that first visit with the Chancellor's people. That joy presented some fears, as he knew somehow that he'd never make it to the Port of Ullapool in the Northern Highlands, and he knew he would never walk the prehistoric stone ways in the isle and the beach.

He felt the missing places of Scotland in some dreams. The 5000-year-old stone circles on the Isle of Lewis grew near him at night. Even Babylon was not yet built when these ancient stone masons, neither Scottish nor British, leveraged their placements in the earliest of Neolithic times. And what a sense of pity he felt, making all those millions in offices and at desks, when he could not reach Callanish. Instead, he read about these achievable places, noting that Ullapool would become a major port. He could imagine joining Walt Whitman on their ferry to the outer isles from Ullapool, mostly because he liked how the word felt in his mouth during dreams. While Ullapool may have become a major tourist place, with a central part of town full of cars, he did not want to know this.

Instead, he thought about the Chancellor, so close to Stirling Bridge, and found past emotions grand. Anyone can walk in a single day up there; back in the days of Wordsworth and the Romantics, you would walk a week up there in Scotland and not pass a single human who asked you your occupation.

LECTURING AT
ST. ANDREWS

He said "no" to the offer of a formal lecture, and instead chose to visit faculty at their home or office. He visited St. Andrews only a few years after Prince William, Britain's future king, had studied there in 2001.

The sheer grandeur of its ancient isolation made it a secure place for a future king. It was a place many American writers visited across time. It was really a college town, on the coast of Fife. Was it the long open spacious cemetery that made it special, or its leatherbound library of books? Would he accept a teaching offer there? Never.

He had become too modern to live a life with a grand past. Location mattered to his working mind, as writer and as businessperson. Aware that the ruined St. Andrew's Cathedral was once one of the top five great pilgrim spots in medieval Europe—akin for visiting Christians to

England far more spacious Canterbury Cathedral and its sister Santiago de Compostela in greater Spain, he would abstain from living there too long, as he was a fish outside now of the paradise of academia in all its forms.

It was with the same restraint that he did not whole-heartedly pursue the Bantle Chair at Syracuse University. After a week of interviews in the Forestry School, the Management School, the Maxwell School of Public Affairs, and the Law School, he was glad they did not give the endowed chair to anyone that year—and kept looking. He was a person who kept forgetting his pass codes to academia. He was a professional whose life was made with books, but he was all about aligning money, people, and rules, not just the books about those things.

Scotland reminded him of all that.

MR. PLUMER,
HIS TEACHER

Travel was absorbing like a grand book. Yet time in his past kept resurfacing even in the grandest of days. As he edged closer to the end of his life, he began to think more about the teachers who had given him his first legs, his initial standing. Without them, he might have proved a solid lawyer or a good surgeon or a rural banker. With Plumer, he became himself.

"Mr. Plumer was not a plumber!" He woke up one morning, saying this out loud to a startled Varlissima. This is what the class had called him—"a plumber"—when they were being mean and hurtful.

Charles Plumer was ahead of his time, and special, and rather strange for the average high school teacher. Outrage was often the start of what mattered to him. But those who got the method to Plumer's manner felt the pressure and the spray within their growing minds.

He taught Latin and great books. But it didn't really matter what Mr. Plumer taught. All truly great teachers teach love of life. The students swam with him in an atmosphere of dense, playful words—plenty of words, and for free.

Over time, Plumer's statements about writing created a set of higher facts. He claimed that at its best, writing was like building a house. Each great paragraph he fluted had a floor, a stairwell, some walls, and a set of bright, well-framed windows to the world.

One day, out of the blue, Plumer said, "It takes two floors to make a story." Having grown up in a small, two-floored home near the railroad tracks, he knew exactly what his teacher meant. The best stories have several floors and are rarely linear, despite what so many teachers required. The best stories draw the reader into the future by creating a presence that allows a sense of the past. The best stories create a mansion of meanings.

He could run up Plumer's arguments all day long, sniffing for hints like a dog on a stairwell, and then jump back down them swiftly, without hurting himself.

This was how he learned that teaching was about extending one's reach. Plumer's stories always led to another story, and then another. This was how Plumer had taught early experimentation with vast mansions of meaning.

In the end, he owed his sense of architectonics in writing to Charles Plumer. He learned that he could build a structure that was like memory itself, and as magical as life itself—if he pushed the Pause and Fast Forward buttons enough. Charles Plumer taught him what mattered:

the sound of the words, and the ability to outrage. Plumer saw eye to eye with the greats, like Twain and Melville, in both anger and in hope.

He related to Plumer as if he had been his lost father. When he was fifteen years old, Plumer had told him out of the blue that he would be a good father someday. Now that he was much older he realized what an insightful risk that proved.

Charles Plumer did not help him remember formulas or see the stars more clearly or even appreciate Shakespeare. Plumer helped him develop a spirit of observation, a sense of belonging anywhere—that is, wherever he felt at play.

OLD AGE AT THE
LOTOS CLUB

The late great Tom Wolfe invited him to join The Lotos Club in 2012. But it took until after Tom's death for him to realize his old age there. Were it not for The Lotos Club, and its distinct company of friends, old age might have proven dreary at times. But whenever he felt he needed to jazz up his calm at Old Stone Church, he'd hop on a train to Manhattan, and make his way to 5 East 66th Street. It was from there a quick walk to Central Park, with its buzz of hills achievable at any age. And visiting the Frick Collection always worked to give him a tick up, as did visiting the shows at the Armory. "There was a very long afternoon to life if you could visit such a club," he thought.

Thanks to Charles Plumer's training, he had been inducted as a member of Mark Twain's Lotos Club in

Midtown Manhattan in his fifties, right after *Doing More with Less* became listed as a *New York Times* bestseller. It took a good while and a set of trips down to the club to even realize what all this meant to his life and the rest of his life as a writer.

From factory boy to member of this elite literary club, he never changed. It was his perception of others that matured. While he had a bad habit of dropping names to make his public talks dramatic and people based, rather than concept based, he now had the chance to watch people whose life achievements made his efforts sensible. He had always felt exactly like a stranger in the paradise of academia, but at this club he felt he had a home away from home.

He was always the same guy from Long Island, always the kid who'd grown up near the railroad tracks, but he needed to work out the boastfulness that business had built and hardwired into him. In business, you get more chances by being bold; but in the life of the mind, in the day to day at the club, it might prove the reverse. It was the perception of others that had ripened so much in him, adding a quiet humility when he sat in the internal garden of the Frick, eyeing real wealth. This was humility at its best.

Now he was among many accomplished people at the club, and from time to time they helped him ready for old age. This was the real value in its membership to him, not the fine welcomes, fresh meals, and outstanding rooms. Now the richness was mostly in a conversation with a few accomplished people, who didn't need to ask for anything, but instead lived lives of a quieter resolution, with tea in the afternoon. He now had many fine talks at noon, where he listened to Robert Caro recall state dinners and tell tales of President Johnson, and heard Gay Talese and Tom Wolfe reinvent the New Journalism, as both memory and achievement.

The process of being proposed, elected, and then honored lasted over a year, and involved secretly solicited reviews of both character and ambition. Since he never felt that he'd be elected, that year passed in pleasant travel for work and discovery. But becoming a member changed everything for him, as it worked its magic and he went from ceaselessly wanting to mostly enjoying watching the members talk.

The first time he entered this place of beautiful stillness and history he came upon the bust of Mark Twain, which stared across the first lounge at a painting of the same author. He was sure this placement of the two Twains was very deliberate.

"How appropriate," he could hear Charles Plumer saying. Plumer did not admire the accomplished as much as appreciate them, in all their human frailty. "Is it not true that accomplished writers are always looking at themselves?" Plumer whispered in his ear.

He experienced one of those near-death dreams that prepared him for a deeper and more wondrous old age . . . What he remembered best about Charles Plumer was a final class in Latin. It proved his first rite of passage into a writer's life. The class had spent most of the spring translating the poetry of Catullus, Homer, and Ovid, and Cicero's Orations. That day, Plumer had taken out some replicated maps showing a Roman hunting camp from 300 AD.

Even in his eighties, he could picture the scene vividly. He was sitting behind Mary Beth, whose left shoulder carried a most lovely "you-need-to-stroke-this" beauty mark. The camp caught his eye over Mary Beth's contoured and tanned teenage shoulder.

Mimicking the posture and tone of a Roman instructor, Plumer held up a photo of a decorative tile from the hunting camp and said, "Now, ever-earnest Dr. Piasecki, please translate this image before us, and render it from Latin into English for the awaiting class." The request clinched his future as a writer, right then and there.

"The woman's rotund butt was naked," he said in his head. He knew the translation was accurate, but he also felt that he was in the middle of a Fellini film, watching as many others watched him. He loved this feeling, the words in his head.

He could see the translation in his head, but could he say it out loud? Finally, he said loudly, "The woman's rotund butt is naked." The class roared. He was a star.

Part Three
AT OLD STONE CHURCH

(VIGNETTES OF THE MAGIC IN OLD AGE)

Eighty! I can hardly believe it . . . My father, who lived to 94, often said that the 80s had been one of the most enjoyable decades of his life. He felt, as I begin to feel, not a shrinking but an enlargement of mental life and perspective. One has had a long experience of life, not only one's own life, but others', too. One has seen triumphs and tragedies, booms and busts, revolutions and wars, great achievements and deep ambiguities, too. . . One is more conscious of transience and, perhaps, of beauty . . . I do not think of old age as an ever grimmer time that one must somehow endure and make the best of, but as a time of leisure and freedom, freed from the factitious urgencies of earlier days, free to ex-

plore whatever I wish, and to bind the thoughts and

feelings of a lifetime together . . ."

—Oliver Sacks

Excerpt from The Joy of Old Age. (No Kidding.),
The New York Times, July 6, 2013

THE MAGIC OF OLD AGE

He began to spend more of each day on legacy. In business he felt if you wanted it done right you best do it yourself first, and maybe a dozen times, before handing it off for rapid replication. But in book writing, each book had to have its own unique crust. And in legacy work, like with the foundation work, it was more about using the wisdom of old age to project a life you wanted, rather than had.

He felt this the most in looking at his home, not his books. Our homes live long after us. As we age, our homes become our core, our deepest sense of self. They become a statement of our trust in the future, what we leave behind for our loved ones.

A home's revealing tone remains as basic and essential and as common as moisture to a plant.

It is easier to study mating outside the home than nesting in the home. What mattered to Bruce now was the survival of his home, Reverend O. J. Bentley's Revolutionary farm estate. His home enabled the growth in his family and friends, as it now housed a foundation that would live after him.

Humans move about a lot more than plants, but they are like plants to the sun of their own memories. A good home absorbs those memories.

In housing our families properly, we experience something both ancient and modern. Homes house our longing and our remorse—things far more important, in the end, than cash or blame. These housed memories are succession manifests, our emotions written large on a canvas that lasts. Homes shape our children. Homes foster an answer to their fears.

Perhaps this is why many cultures call the nexus of land and property "an estate and a living trust." Of course, a trust is a specific legal instrument that allows an estate to bypass probate and pass directly to the individual selected. But the many cultures that see higher facts in this arrangement know it is about much more than tax relief. In this way, a text is very much like a home.

In old age he realized at last a lasting thing: the world's most beautiful and exceptional books are like mansions.

A book, then, is a large, sustained interconnected statement of trust, a chosen display of our shared faith in a near future. Every book holds within it a stern proposition: "Come into my home."

PAINKILLERS
AND MEDICINES

On February 16, 2023, he had his left knee totally replaced by Dr. Marc Fuchs at Albany Medical Center. His tightly aligned team included a caring total knee coordinator, a resident nurse who taught a class on what to expect, through to the hospital team who put him into dream through a spinal and a leg nerve block. When he woke two hours later his mind was clear and he was ready to walk with a walker and his wife to a car parked like all citizens park at the hospital.

This was so different than his first knee replacement seven years before. Modern medicine has advanced in eliminating the days in the hospital, the bags of blood at his side, and his need for total pain relief. This time at age sixty-eight he did it without a need for opioids, neither oxycodone nor tramadol. While the doctor has prescriptions filled for both drugs, he felt he contained his pain through stretching and ice, through Celebrex as the anti-inflammation friend, and simple Tylenol as the pain numbing over the counter aid.

Basketball knees often require painkillers and meds. He felt in youth as if he could fly through the air; and even forty-eight minutes were within range of doing the improbable in terms of competition and winning, flying into three hundred pounds of muscle, or slapping his wrist on the baseline drive. By the time he was at Cornell, he had shattered his right kneecap, and injured the left as well. Only time could tell him about consequence.

When he first met his wife, he was stretching his post-surgical knee on crutches on Hamilton Street in Ithaca. The stunning redhead said to him, under her soft breath, "mobility is a gift," walking her friends' dog, Ceres. He knew he was lucky in that injury. His hippo-campus said through the knee pain: "I'll have to keep her around," sort of like a caveman says in his cave when he has extra meat frying.

Jump ahead a few decades, with plenty of hobbling near her on hikes, to age sixty-eight, where she is the aid to his Zimmer implant, the girl who could help him get through the pain. He did this without opioids because she was there, refusing to allow him to shut down his central nervous system like last time, and sink into depression.

Well back when he was sixty, the opioids for severe pain felt like a Mack truck sat on his elevated self, where he struggled for four or five hours in fog and sleep. Now he got up with a clear head on the hour, every hour, the first days, to avoid blood clots and overmedication.

He left the same day, like so many others now, on the mend with minimal meds. He avoided blood clots and infection and any complications of compromise of flexibility. He took inspiration from this change of knees. He began to reimagine aging more Cicero-like. First you start with the straightforward and obvious, then you go to the consequential like family and wife, and then you end with a bang if you can.

When you avoid painkillers and meds the bang is felt in different more alive ways. You ask, Who put this possibility into the universe? It was a new kind of swoosh.

Some of these joys of survival and pain relief became more permanent and more common in his older years. It was embodied in a complete Samurai outfit he once saw in Dallas. As he visited his Texan billionaire, Trammel Crow, on assignment, the meaning of the armor became his. His job was to bring a few odd bird executives to this odd bird graduate of Yale, to his town hall to celebrate the world's largest earth day. He did this earning a rate beyond imagination, as he serves those thirty-five global clients in BNSF and Toyota. It began to make sense to him. Wealth can bring any kind of thing to your neighborhood.

Trammel's brother was a fantastic collector of Asian Art. In fact he filled in the Dallas Arts District on 2010 Flora Street, and for the world at www.crowcollection. org, many Asian masterpieces. But dealing with the brother billionaire on his own books, and his own leaders, was an entirely otherworldly trip. When Trammel invited him into his historic home, he felt fierce loyalty. He felt like the complete Samurai crow collection, exquisitely crafted and perfectly preserved by wealth and access. Yet what distinguished his armor was words, created outside himself and travelling to many places.

A TOUCAN
IN TUSCANY

The austere beauty in a Tuscan hill, any hill outside of Florence, he found similar to an italics in any well written sentence. It stood out. Special unto itself, the beauty in Tuscany—you will feel it—is austere and simple. The rest of the paragraph spun the tale, but it was the italics that focused the soul for comprehension.

He travelled with this sense of composition, and the elements of style, whenever he roamed Europe. Struck by the magnificence of the Italian countryside, Edith Wharton wrote in 1904 her *Italian Villas and Their Gardens,* as she was building her master location in Lenox, Massachusetts. (My copy is blessed with pictures and illustrations by Maxfield Parrish in a new edition that has become classical on my shelf.)

In this beautifully phrased book, read on planes visiting Tuscany, Wharton promised him this: "Utility was doubtless not the only consideration which produced this careful proportioning of the Villa off the garden—all this was taken into account by a race of artists who studied the contrast of aesthetic emotions as keenly as they did the juxtaposition of dark cypress and pale lemon tree, of deep shade and level sunlight."

Overall, Wharton is right, he felt. But then something happened on another visit.

One day he saw a toucan in Tuscany that brought all this into sudden suspicion. It was not unlike Hawthorne's moment with the *Marble Faun,* but more modern. Toucans, those large beaked beauties, belong in Brazil or the jungles of Peru. They are tropical, but can be imported, like fine coffees, into Tuscany. But should they?

Here remained his argument. The beauty in the Tuscan hills has remained livable for centuries, resisting overdevelopment and urbanization, gently near all the great public art, but also withdrawn while performing, a magic balance of distance and detail. Pardon the pun, but you do not descend in Tuscany. You only ascend from the Arno.

One afternoon, while ascending from Florence into the hills, with the professor of management who had spent the prior summer translating his book *World Inc* into Italian, he spotted—while walking as she took a call, this toucan in Tuscany.

He saw the bird through a beautiful villa porch window. The glass old but without streaks or stains, the garden austere but detailed. In bold green and yellow, the bird refused to rest its captive beak, and instead chose to peck at its branch in the cage, asking him to question everything he had ever witnessed or read about in Tuscany.

It was a moment of sudden wrongness, to flip Wallace Stevens on his fanny. Italy cannot be captured by a jar, or a juniper, or by an imported bird. He felt insulted, in the wrong place.

What makes a Tuscan hill is its complete simplicity of emotion; the ways the Villas last in ways that the family farm meets the garden. Free from an excess of flowers, the garden meets the home. But there was the toucan, eyeing him as the foreign visitor.

In his notebooks, over the decades, he noticed that most entries of his travels when in Italy had italics in a passage, as if the feeling of this complete rightness could be captured by special emphasis. Suddenly, he began to question this use of italics. But a descent into blandness was also wrong.

"A dream you dream alone is only a dream," noted John Lennon at his peak. "But a dream you dream with others is reality." Perhaps what was off was the company, the villa owner and the translator.

Was this translator dreaming my words in Italian, or only faking some of it? Was this colorful toucan on the porch real or a rude fluke, allowed by an excess of wealth with total disregard of everything else totally surrounding this Villa? His moment of sudden wrongness turned around in him.

The toucan looked as healthy as if it had just arrived from Peru. In his imagination, he called the bird King

Ben Tat. He watched it, the translator's call was long and passionate. The bird tapped its large beak at him as if gesturing through the window. He was alone with his observation of wrongness, but he had not then power— as in the best nightmares—to move an inch of change onto the bird or the setting. He was at the wrong place at the wrong time in the best of Italy.

Perhaps it was the bird. Toucans are like the Grinch who stole Christmas, as out of place as Horton in his miniature universe, as special as Yertle the Turtle. Yet the toucan could not fly away, like he would later that week, leaving his book on shelves for people he never met.

Without conversing with the Tuscan villa owners, he could contemplate what came next. The bird would get mangy. Not dirty, nor disgusting, nor filthy, simply mangy like an old, loved but dying dog in Venice. The owner, sipping her dark limp drink near the bird, seemed to him now keenly alone. His emotions sank at the thought that many would buy his book in Italian but not understand where he came from.

While toucans in the wild are wildly social, this toucan, like its owner, was alone. It was intimidating to see how the Mediterranean warmth suited the bird. Popular in the forests of Central and South America, this is one of the world's loudest, noisiest birds—its song sounds like a frog in a long slow croaking. But this bird in Tuscany sat in silence. That is what bothered him the most, as he could hear the translator chatting away. He felt as alone as a book at sea.

In the wild, toucans can toss fruit at each other. That is the joy he felt in a primal way when he tossed his basketball swiftly between teammates. But hunters now have captured the game and the bird as pets, and fly them to the wealthy in every continent, warm and cold.

Knowing all this, he decided never again to feel melancholy in Italy. He would never again ask to meet his translators.

A LIGHTER TIME
IN LUCCA

He found the beauty in Tuscan style was in the little things, not Rome's magnificent waterfalls, and sports complexes of old. It was like the beauty he found in a woman's face, or a child's smile. It was not about the repressed reserved elements in the style, it was about the overall gentle and persuasive presentation, the authentic passion in the place. Lucca's leather-making region was only a small part of this medieval walled town, walkable in half a day, and wonderful in all detail.

Less than an hour outside of Florence airport, Lucca is a hidden treasure. He was invited to Lucca for four days before Thanksgiving, to meet managers and to give a speech for the billionaire owner of Sofidel, the paper conglomerate.

While up on the stage, awaiting his turn, he watched the owner of the firm with his two sons on each side of him, in the front row, with a thumbs up or a thumbs down depending on what the announcer said. He was so expressive, unable to sit still like a church goer.

Would this happen to him as he spoke? As he talked to the audience, moderated by an Italian TV personality on a white leather couch, he thought about the lovely town church the billionaire rented for the business conference. And then he began to talk in slow methodical English.

"Doing More with Less" was on the cover of the event brochure, and it was their motto for the "conversation." While away longer than he first wanted from family that holiday, he enjoyed the time in Lucca, and promised to find ways to get back to buy a wallet.

COLETTE AT NIGHT, AGAIN

Although he was now seventy-two, he was at times so world-weary, in the purely physical sense, that he depended on his daughter to chauffeur him around on most of the nights she was in town. This was good for her, but better for him—and best for the other drivers out there. Saratoga knew to beware of his wide turns, and his absent-minded driving patterns. He was not so much dangerous as unpredictable, Colette reported.

When he would take a miserable turn, he was often thinking of a great passage from Shakespeare. A history of failure to stop properly filled his driving record. He saw a secret correlation between his speeding violations and the number of times per year he now received a note about being anthologized: it was an inverse ratio. This thought made him smile.

Varlissima had grown tired of his self-absorption and seldom ventured out with him to greet these new publics. He had traveled widely on book tours, on consulting gigs, and Varlissima rarely joined him—saving travel with him for vacations. After college, Colette would join him on the more exotic tours when she could, sometimes with her husband, and later with her kids. He would always travel with a laminated rolled-up version of the picture from her high school graduation party, as if in holding time still, he was safer somehow.

Occasionally, a professional literary secretary would drive him around to these work obligations, dressed mostly in humble black skirts, with her stunning black hair pulled back in a ponytail. Folks came to recognize her—she often made them smile. In recognizing her, they recognized him, who now walked slower than before, and with more of the invisibility of posture and pace that come with advanced age.

Now, at night, he was more content than seemed possible from his prior years of travel. All it took was a book and a set of memories to fall into a deeper sleep. The art of giving talks, he found, was like the art of newspaper writing. You stroked all the platitudes from your best passages, with a touch of humor, until they started to purr. He remained popular in his public outreach well into his seventies.

THE DRAGON ARUM

By his early eighties, he realized that anything of worth in the twenty-first century had already been destroyed by the Internet. While speed had become the order of the day, he knew that many things, like the magnificent black lily—that dragon arum—require time to bloom. Most days, there was impatience surrounding every-thing, from the details of a date to the reactions to a great movie.

Yet 80 percent of the century remained. Instead of the tragedy of *Romeo and Juliet* there was the wonder of Avatar, where flying beasts and creatures with extended legs embodied early love and longing, vying against a machine too big to turn off. Gladiatorial combat had morphed into the beautiful and improbable archery of Katniss Everdeen in *The Hunger Games*.

Technology had evolved so rapidly that everyone could play fast and loose with time: youth could see lurid shows meant for adults, and adults could settle into the fantasy of endless youth. For many, it was becoming harder and harder to turn away from the immediacy of the screen and recall actual literary experience—except for the back-to-the-earth folks who still had a backyard to roam in.

Only books could still create the sense of forgiveness and hope.

The dragon arum was a mighty strange late bloomer in his back garden—its long, oily black pistil was surrounded by a lush, deep red, almost powdery petal that caressed the pistil with close care, despite rain or storm or torture by the gardener. Privately, he had tested his dragon arums many times, trying to separate the spears from their case, but it was useless. If you broke one you broke them both. By now he felt the same way about himself and Varlissima.

It fascinated him how people made their couple-hood into something dramatic. This much was true: he and Varlissima had been late bloomers. But many couples that survive are late bloomers. There is so much red and black in lovers, so much magic in the fit of the pistil and the surrounding petals, that survival seems as much a matter of luck and attitude as anything.

So he paid little heed to those who assigned so much wattage to his coupling with Varlissima. He knew that Colette was the magical glue that had kept them together: she was the gift that had taken fortune's might and caressed it into a greater calm than harm. She was the girl made woman, as he was the man-made old man. He began to wonder what life might have been like if he had not fathered Colette.

He came to like new neighbors and new books, and it was almost as good to meet them as to remember them. Otherwise, the weight of his mother's absence proved too much. The expected downs of old age lessened whenever he was with people—and at Old Stone Church, this turned out to be often. His yard remained large and inviting. A good book is a great leveler, and a great book is a good way to silence the neighbors.

Sure, he had always pushed himself onto half of humanity, but this was how he had earned attention—how he had decided not to die too early, like his father. He would not give up that persistence, that conversational curiosity.

He was beginning to drop his defenses, to let in some wondrous, Marquez-like pirates at the gate. Until now, he had been jealous and controlling when it came to his reputation. But he really had nothing left to defend, except fun itself. His addiction to adding to the good yielded some excesses. His offices were filled with idiosyncratic icons, gifts from visitors from around the world. He groped and clutched these icons, cluttering his life with them as Freud had, in his artifact-cramped office on Vienna's Ringstrasse.

He had his village. He had his jungle. He had in summer robust gardens—full of blue mouse ears that did not talk back, clusters of simple pure hearts, and abiqua drinking gourds, whose intense blue edges and emerald-green centers made him smile, both because he found their combination of colors so unexpected, and because their absorption of rain was so clever and so certain. Even with his diminishing eyesight, he still loved the petunias of his past, and still wanted his spring to bloom at Old Stone Church.

Ironically, almost magically, his surroundings at the end resembled surroundings at his start, except for all the wealth. He was with women. He was with nature. He was a man open and outside. It was all very much like living near the Long Island Railroad tracks, surrounded by women.

He was getting ready for the final resolution and choice.

SUCCESS AT HOME

For at least two decades, he had been preparing to die at sea. That would fit the image of the drunken Hercules, and set sail to the notion that he was merely a fortunate homebody who had made good. During several trips overseas, he had eyed a piece of land near the coast of Sicily, and near the same hill that Virgil had climbed every summer to escape the disease of the coastal swamps.

Varlissima had eyed the same town—Erice, just up the hill from Trapani, where all the homes had both bad plumbing and out-of-this-world views. These homes were made from the same magical, beautiful, locally quarried Sicilian stone. "Strong and steady," they thought, each time they visited these stone homes. Everyone was in rare agreement: Colette saw that the town was special. They all felt "the surprise" there.

At eighty-three, limping on the cobblestones that led up to this small plaza with a spectacular view, he was allowed to buy—with Varlissima's approval—their second stone home. At his advanced age, the grand sameness of all these homes would lead him, several times, to visit the wrong home, where he would end up in delightful unintended conversations, usually in English.

He and Varlissima settled near the top of the hill from which Virgil had watched the wars of Peloponnese. On some nights, as they sat together, they could watch ships nearing the coast, much as Virgil did in his recollections of the North African and Greek positioning in ancient wars.

"Adventure is gratuitous unless brought home for sharing." He came to thank Herman Melville for having taught him that. As he wandered to exotic places, he always brought them back to Old Stone Church Road. Thoughts of Erice were more like memories of a vacation than experiences of a second home. There was no second home, in fact, except on the balance sheets.

He had first gotten the idea of appropriating the world when he visited Sigmund Freud's Vienna home: it was filled with the totems that the doctor would then shred to pieces, stuffing them back into his most mesmerizing theories and books.

Success at home, he now saw, was about bringing the world within his own boundary conditions. And intelligence was about feeling good about that—feeling accomplished by being scaled back into satisfaction.

He did not, in the end, need the full world; all he really needed was a good place from which to compose his world. The persistence to get past home while at home was the ultimate key.

At eighty-eight, he imagined himself placing the two numbers for infinity next to each other. The number eighty-eight made sense. He was ready to die that year, but he did not. It took great persistence, this aging process, where urine and digestion and standing straight become big things. All of this proved tolerable for someone who stayed true to his home.

He and Varlissima kept the Bentley estate for their child, for her children, and for her children's children, just as the Bentleys had done for seven generations before them. This proved rare in the new America, but it was something he had wanted from the first time he heard Uncle Ziggy talk about the old country.

By good fortune, he returned many times to his home on Old Stone Church Road. The lawn looked better than ever before. Was it the new forms of targeted fertilizer? Or was it simply his failing eyesight?

At a dinner party for his eighty-ninth birthday, the lovely Varlissima slipped a strange quote from D. H. Lawrence into the proceedings, reading it aloud with a knowing quiver in her eyebrows:

> *I can never decide whether my dreams are the result of my thoughts, or the thoughts are the result of my dreams. It is very queer. But dreams make conclusions for me. They decide things finally. I dream a decision. Sleep seems to hammer out for me the logical conclusions of my vague days, and offer me them as dreams.*

Having survived him for so many decades, Varlissima was saying, in her wonderful indirect way, that she had come to see that most of his life he was not decisive as much as a dreamer—and that, perhaps, is what she had loved in him.

THE LAST OBSESSION

The last obsession involves the face of death, time's most constant mistress and its final formidable friend. He could not out-talk her, he could not out-walk her. He must lie next to her, and watch his remaining breaths.

Decades of action repress the fear of death; this was why, he believed, some of his peers remained addicted to business long after having gained sufficient wealth. But she resurfaces, mocking us with her silk see-through pantaloons. Even those born with grace and force cannot outlast her fascination.

He already knew that many are hurt—and had found ways to say, with Emily Dickinson, "But what of that?" He already knew that life is short. But again, what of that?

Despite all this, he witnessed the pursuit of a new equation: investments in genetic means of extending life, the restoration of broken limbs, the search for new ways to get even, to shimmy off her pantaloons and say, "Ha, I told you I could outwit you." But, near the end, he knew that none of this could be sustained, and that death was impossible to master.

Some call the fascination with death the source of all creative effort. Others size her up as if a fine Elizabethan clock, that mocks us as it ticks away.

Like Jung, he found his wealth in an understanding of death's many costumes. His final obsession told him that the Book of Job is open to its most haunting chapters beneath most business dealings, beside most intimate relationships, and in every honest memoir. Death is the dance that none can outlast.

Yet the beach where he was born suggested that he might live on in his works, in the dreams of his daughter, in his hopes for a faultless company succession.

So much of his wealth had seemed contingent, once, on his own enterprising will, and the grace of good fortune. So much of him seemed dispersed in memories now. In the end, no savvy investment advisor or brilliant estate attorney had any lasting answer. They were as ineffective, despite their big fees, as Job's friends.

Half the trouble with this obsession was caused by the will—the force that had driven him into his fantasy of near futures in the first place. However fascinated by will or intrigued by endless, receding horizons, all must pay the fee to cross over to another shore. Varlissima was the one he had elected to be by his side.

He knew all this at first: before college, before competition, before success. But he waited for her to confirm it in him. There had been so much pleasure in pretending to forget this last obsession.

This last obsession brought him back, in the end, to Old Stone Church. He was at home in this place; he knew its winds and its history, and that it was his part of the world. Varlissima remained his wonder woman at Old Stone Church because she had liberated this last obsession in him from the start, even during his first days with her at Cornell, knowing his defiant youth to be his answer to the nearing face of death. He had come to believe that she had stuck with him for all those decades because he was willing to forge ahead, and embrace each day with her.

He could see the face of death more clearly now, without distraction. She came constantly nearer each day, to shave him even, and to clip his ever-harder toenails. He could feel her satisfy him, eating him to the core with her stare of disapproval or her smile. Either brought him close to the same end. And while he hated this obsession, he knew that its splendidly focused, incredible rightness would win.

GOOD READING

The simple acknowledgment of aging can be as swift as it is severe. It was impossible to repel: age continued to attack, like Mongol invaders whose round eyes never seemed to sleep.

After a while, all the insults of aging looked the same: insistent. He was no sultan after all, neither in business nor in life, despite the land holdings and his vast-imagined legacy. He was simply another man, and an old one at that. Consciously and willingly, he entered the final seasons.

He knew that life would carry on in his absence. Little on his property would be affected by his death. The money tree would likely remain standing, or most of it. The butterfly garden would continue to bloom in the spring, amid the sound of the peepers and the katydid's soulful song.

Throughout his decades at Old Stone Church, the five winds of change had lifted the descending leaves—sometimes for as long as ten minutes—into the chilled air of his back gardens; but eventually they would fall, only to rise again before hitting the ground, along with their muted and identical sisters. There was no real, lasting human lesson in watching the leaves fall. There was no real value in counting the blades of grass each spring. The home and the church were his answer.

Varlissima had warned him not to get too attached to this home. She said they needed to be prepared to sell it at any time; for if it became too big to maintain, she would kill him before the house killed her!

He now remembered Varlissima's prediction, as they signed their mortgage a few months before Colette's birth. She said the home would witness the three inevitable stages of every couple's sex life: first there is house sex, when they are newly infatuated with the place and have sex all over the house. Then there is bedroom sex, when they allow the routine only in the bedroom to protect the children. The final stage, she predicated, is hall sex—when they've been married so long they just pass each other in the hallway and shout, "Fuck you!"

He looked for his antecedents under the soles of his boots, and never found them except when at home. Walt was not his father after all, but a smart hint at what a father could be. Wordsworth's child of man was only intimation, another form of transfiguration. It all became a matter of degrees, of vital signs and small differences, amid a vast universe of similarities in what was claimed to be humanity.

There was now so much more than mere humanity available in his backyard.

THE WIND IN HIS
BACKYARD

There were five corners to his property. The Old Stone Church, his home itself, the company offices, and the old barn were peaked by a fifth corner where the prior owner's wife had constructed a small building to sing her operas. These five corners defined the property from which he did his earning, growing, and sharing.

These five corners produced the winds of change that had always stood strong behind him—waving him on, tempting a boy from West Islip to ask the bigger questions—while the Old Stone Church stood solid, defying his tiny ambition with its stone certainty. The uneven rock face reminded him, daily, that it, not he, was proud testimony to the passing of even the strongest winds. It had stood there, quietly, since 1824.

There was something deep and astonishing about wind—something that kept him going, pushing him from behind, something that did not destroy his hope. It said: *"Fervor is more important than fame, zeal more worthy than worth."* He had never read this in a book, yet he felt this mantra deep as part of his heart, pumping his blood.

Wind was worldly, event-based, and more mysterious than formal thought. Where once only women dwelled, the wind now formed a source of his inspiration. Whenever sick, he simply found a way outside and sat with the wind, cup of tea in hand, cigar unlit, and soon felt better.

He saw that his proportionate, ego-based self—the self by which he had been measuring his accomplishments and bank-book—had operated under a recurrent, insistent, functional deception, an illusion of certainty, despite the fact that some things are beyond proportion, like wind.

"What if the things that matter most, in the end, are beyond measure? Is that the best way to define God?" he asked.

Boldly overweight and overworked, he stood as if against a final wall that held him up. He leaned into his next thinking—as one leans into the wind when it blows bitter cold.

But this time the wind was warm, and the lean comfortable. He said, "The computational self, the self that measured what mattered in the everyday, that calculated and assigned value to things, had been a strong force in youth"—but as he aged into this new stance, he began to round things off and to wonder where wind comes from, and why it is usually there, but invisible, subtle, and intractable. There are even winds, he felt now, that only follow rivers.

He loved all this whirling around the Old Stone Church: the simple way the wind spoke to him in the fall and winter—shaking his trees, and at times threatening to bring down the old twisted limbs and trunk of the money tree, but never really bothering to do it.

Life was now all about his backyard; it was all about the wind, about the wind's temporary resistance to the deeper meanings that meant we were alive.

FURTHER READING
ABOUT THE WORLD

He was traveling a great deal less now, so his retreat into memory mounted . . .

He remembered the scene in Vienna vividly—the slow inquiring pace with which she approached. She was nameless; he was in his twenties. He could remember every curve of her shape, the length of her shaven thighs, the bones of her hips that protruded beyond her flat belly, the beauty mark on her neck—such an odd place—that spoke his language. But all he could recall of her clothes was that she was not dressed in the ugly reds of America. She had perfect lips, perfect hips, and a neck worth holding.

She was able to press her lips against the glass of his Viennese friend's car, and not speak his language, yet still seduce. How was all this possible? How could he have lived through all that past, that long sensual middle, and still be around to think about it all again?

When he held her neck now in memory, he knew that true leaders were self-appointed. Gandhi in India was not the same man as Gandhi in his memoirs or at home. Nelson Mandela in South Africa was not the same man in his memoirs or at the United Nations. Distortion is inevitable as we move through time—this self-invention, this revision, this delightfully windy sense of self and self-worth. If you repress this wind at the center of fervor, you can never be free, never create something the world did not know how to ask for.

The sun spoke to him through all this mist. She whispered something in his ear. She whipped her chin, with a foreign smile, and began down the road toward the Ringstrasse, never to be with him again until just now.

She must have originally been from a deeper cast—perhaps Russian or a mix of Russian and Asian. Her name sounded to him, that day in Vienna, like Maya. His friend let her in and left the car; the rest was memory. All his readings in history could not dispel her, could not alarm her, could not warm her; and all his learning did not need to erase her.

Another of his memories would rise from the bed and brush her teeth afterwards, another had bad feet, a third wore hats that were about ten times the worth of her jeans, which she flung to the floor without request or longing.

Memories were becoming great books—immensely pleasurable, but now also far off, as if beyond the importance of the actual people who first wrote them. A shelf could seem miles away these days. When he looked over the books of those he had met: Gay Talese with the tall tales of his immigrant father; Tom Wolfe with his bold and flamboyantly certain prose; Robert Caro, whose historic detail was as exact and recurrent as the movements of a trained swimmer—they seemed decades away now. He would get up from his reading to reach for another, knees cracking.

Good reading became his best mistress.

SELDOM SEEN
IN SARATOGA

The paper-thin katydids returned faithfully each summer to the trees lining Old Stone Church Road.

Remorse was his favorite emotion because its half-life was long—longer in its screeching certainties than the katydids' eggs that hide on the bark of the twigs in his backyard. The tiny nymphs hatch each spring, and most find mates mathematically, as they mature in the heat and moisture that gathers near Saratoga during the dog days of late summer.

The katydids danced outside his living room windows, making loud, screeching, protest sounds. Seldom seen in Saratoga, they were populous at his homestead.

True to their name, these *Pterophylla camellifolia* were normally camouflaged in the many large oaks near Old Stone Church. If he listened hard at night, he could discern their song, even over the relentless peepers in the pond next door.

Like most relatives of grasshoppers and crickets, the true katydids are best known for the call of the males, bolder than Shakespeare's Hotspur. Loud, rasping notes—worse than teenagers in heat—the bugs would appear in late June, right after his Corporate Affiliates had left town. He was able to be quiet again, then, and listen to the sound coming from the broad-leafed trees. The ground-floor windows were wide open—just as they must have been open in the early years of the house—and some of the katydids would cling to the meshed windows.

By the height of track season in Saratoga, their chorus would become a deafening crescendo that would last throughout the night; but by early fall, only a few males would continue to call. In the cold night air, they seem to call with a delayed and dignified dejection.

The ones still calling were those that had failed to find mates. They would cling to his study windows as he turned off the light. Those rare males were the ones he was most attracted to. Sensing a loss that is not yet there was a rich way to earn winter's alertness, the katydids said to him each summer.

The katydid dies, its bright green wings crossed with the heavy veins of time. You can find the casing near the trees after spring. Meanwhile, the long antenna of remorse lives on.

THE INCREDIBLE
RIGHTNESS
OF RESOLVE

He was ninety-six, alert to the vastness beside him, which he could still glimpse when shopping for books on Manhattan's Upper East Side. He was now thankful, knowing that he could never possibly read what he had acquired.

Books were his native universe—he came to see some as his private deer dances, sending him smoke signals and warnings. He began to sign his name on page ninety-six for fun, as it was his secret page, an ancient signal that would help Colette seek out honest borrowers from book sharks after he was soon gone. Books were, in the end, his portfolio of dreams worth cultivating. He never lent a book without expecting it back. Most other things he gave away with abandon, never expecting them back.

Oscar Wilde had noted that "there is no such thing as a moral or an immoral book. Books are either well-written, or badly written." There was no hero in this library of his, only charming and life-affirming books. Twain was as right as Wilde: "A thick old fashioned heavy book is the finest thing in the world to startle a noisy cat."

With a sense of mounting irony, he also now knew that it was books—not his original family—that had developed his soul for society . . . his final resting place.

HIS SUCCESSION PLANS

Colette had kids, and her kids had kids. His Old Stone Church estate remained his domain, as the generations came by now. Call this dumb luck: it had all become enough.

He was beginning to understand why the best estate plans see three generations out, or more, and he celebrated in his soul their terms for "contingent" generations—what superbly absurd wording for extended financial love.

Something still mattered with a rightness that he wanted to capture and to explain to his descendants. But he could not—except in anecdotes and vignettes— share this valuable something. He would assemble the family, mutter a few things. They still wanted figures and promises from the old man. It was not that they were the three daughters of King Lear. They were merely seeking clarity, which he lacked. Perhaps it was the silencing effects of death herself. So, often, he refused to give too much detail in each account, even to Bonnie Jones, his estate attorney. Varlissima would get red in the face out of embarrassment. He had negotiated the executors, and sometimes changed them on what seemed like a whim.

During recent years, he felt that he had captured, on rare occasions, this elusive guest, this meaning of meanings, when she would visit him at the beach or in his bed with the warm breath of a stallion. He liked this muse of death to visit more and more, her black strength of a ponytail hovering near him. To hell with practicality when she walked near. He felt this way now about the approach of death. She would stand near him until he was satisfied, and then jolt off.

Whitman's gigantic beauty of a stallion all his own up close. Fantasy was physical, at times.

He decided that in coming home, he had been given the best clue to his family's destiny. This made him feel even better than his succession plans and the gifts structured across Colette's children's children's lives. He knew that his money would be felt by them, but he could not really feel them that far out, although he often tried. During his business days he had said "money is meaningless if projected too far," and now he knew the personal depth of that higher fact.

The lightning storm of his recall was refined like an athlete's muscles, transporting him a bit faster and further than ever before, until his universe seemed as if it was passing him by. But he knew, as he walked the coastlines of his finest memories, he knew he would watch Colette's final wave of goodbye soon, as he stood unable to move against that wall of time.

She was his legacy, his final pleasant textual passage to the world.

This, at last, was what made him whole.

HE IMAGINED
HIS READERS

He did not know when he would die. She would call him, this lovely siren, even touch his weaker arm early some mornings with a tingle, asking him to join her and her lovely set of friends.

Each friend would have a new wet curve to dash before him; a new storyline to tempt him. He had learned an important thing: that humankind has not woven the web of life, but that each of us is merely a thread within that greater web. And eventually, he would glide into this stronger, lasting realm, feeling the sticky and sincere connections of life and death itself. Getting to the ancients, becoming one of them during his mature years, was like touching the synapses within his own brain now. He could feel their warmth, their surprising closeness of tradition and change, their sharp corrections from A to

Z in a memory, their constant rewiring, even while he was still alive.

Memory is life's most astute accomplishment.

He could only dream about it, this thing called death, and it added vivid colors to his life, even at ninety-six, and a delirious intensity to his anticipated remaining days. His brain felt, at last, believable.

Every third thought he had now was a memory.

More and more each day, the images that floated in his mind as he rested recalled the sirens calling him into sleep. The logic of lyric filled his days and nights.

They were lovely, these muses of death. They were his newest friends.

COLETTE DISCOVERS THIS MEMOIR

That October morning, her breasts were warm. This muse, however worldly she appeared, wore the rightness of his home inside her. The scent of the musty leaves of Old Stone Church's many oaks and maples were blended with the astral perfumes of this nearing but not nursing muse.

A bad heart, a bad set of eyes, ears half forgotten, and a set of twisted neck nerves—these were the things of his physical life now. Yet his spiritual life, when shared with other people, was at an all-time high. In fact, these higher facts of people and their nature were making him into a man who lived often under the total absorption of a reader lost in a great book.

His plan this day was to reread *The Tempest*. He held in his hand the Folio Society's 450th anniversary edition of the book, designed by a team of giants, to celebrate the Bard's birthday.

The choice allowed him, despite his poor eyesight, to read again about Prospero and his daughter in a relaxed manner, to reread the familiar words without eyes wandering from text to comment, in a fine paper crispness. This made the book itself have the force of a personality, not to mention the words of Shakespeare. Baskerville letterpress type remains one of the most timeless of English typefaces, he felt, and he felt the people of Folio had designed the book for his hands.

It was as if book printer Stan Lane knew Prospero, as well. And it was as if he knew, for sure, that some distinct day, after his death, that his only daughter, Colette, would reread his work while he was gone. The quality of that thought, as he held this particular book, proved poignant to him. They both—the book and the thought—gave him hope, somehow, that Colette would know his work someday.

Varlissima tried to wake him from this reading.

He held on tightly to the long, heavy book.

The marbling effect of the past and the present were like the droplets of oil that floated in the printing solution of carrageen moss that allowed, at the right temperature, this special, dreamlike quality to the paper and the tale.

He'd roam his hand over these book covers during dreamy afternoon naps like he had once roamed the sensual curves of his lovers. Yes, he said to himself—he had been hand marbled by women, making each of his books unique, but all of a human pattern. He was not shaking outside now; he was shaking inside.

He was descending into a depth in tradition that showed him how superficial and wanting all his work remained—that is, superficial if compared to the tradition now in his lap. He was glad that he had left the study of Shakespeare to others. For the study of the Bard could have consumed his entire life, as it did some of his classmates. What mattered now was if Colette might at an older age reread his works. That was all that mattered this day. It was becoming an agitated dream, like the ones he had during those nights when he first dreamt of Frida.

Varlissima was now telling him that this was a special day: Colette would be visiting with her now thirty-year old daughter, Ariel.

But he had fallen into a deep, almost misty sleep, still clutching *The Tempest*.

He was trying, in this dream, to convey something urgent to his daughter, and now to Ariel beside her. His dream became verbal: *"If you have a redemptive imagination, Ariel and Colette, and if you both care to make something out of the rest of your lives, beyond money, and influence, and prestige, you may sense in these books on my shelves some roots to family longevity."*

He had not felt such urgency to get through to his only daughter since she had decided on her first college. He felt, in this dream, that she understood what he meant about a redemptive imagination, and this made him feel warm, and thankful.

. . . He fell into a deeper, hotter sleep, still clinging to *The Tempest*. Colette chatted with Varlissima outside his room. They were drinking jasmine tea. They could still talk, intimately, for hours. He had sometimes been jealous of this mother-to-daughter closeness; but now he felt it all good, and sensible, and even wonderful.

The wind collected outside.

Colette had discovered his memoir the day before. With her mom and daughter near, Colette had flipped through the passages addressed to her in his books. She understood him like never before.

What a persistent bastard he had turned out to be, Varlissima had hinted during that afternoon chat—both to Colette, and surprisingly, to Ariel. He had been suffering from vertigo since 2007, but the family had never let that settle in, as he kept traveling, as he kept earning, as he kept writing for decades after that. This made him hard to live with at times. Perhaps the dream irritation was a result of this advanced vertigo.

After Colette left that night, he deeply regretted missing her and Ariel.

In the middle of that night, he thought vividly about the Japanese portrayal of longevity: three perfectly white cranes—one for family, one for action, and one for memory. Beautifully engraved icons revealed all three to be intimately related. He wished desperately that before he died he could convey to Colette, and perhaps the younger Ariel, the incredible rightness of family, since he knew he never got it right in one spot in any of his books. But now this wrongness felt right, like when finding a glorious passage in a book!

Science would change, profits would wither, friendships might go missing, love itself might prove forgotten; but this figure-eight of family, action, and memory had the promise of our future.

He was so glad he had brought up this idea of a redemptive imagination during Colette's life. He felt it shouldn't be hidden, the way that some parents hide from discussing sex or love itself.

Colette now saw the connections in his work and in his life—she was beginning to know what he had worked so hard to know. She knew as well how little we can capture in a single life, and she came to find he had tried the best he could. She would do the same.

In all this he lived on, feeling again that he had achieved a resolution that might last.

MEMORY IS THE ACCOMPLISHMENT

Professor M. H. Abrams, his mentor at Cornell, never really left his world—as Abrams and his larger self had never, even for a day, left the world of Cornell. The professor had successfully converted his physical body into a word body. That is, he found a way to phrase a set of lasting words, a world view, if you will, that could be passed on to folks like Harold Bloom of Yale, and many others like himself, with little distortion or fabrication. This conversion, this transformation of the physical self into a social self, was the greatest lesson he had learned while at Cornell. It would be done through hard work, and creative persistence. Without first having that example in Abrams—and a few others, like the poet Archie Ammons, also from Goldwin Smith Hall—he might have remained a factory kid, making tools that lasted the test of time, not books.

Almost eight decades ago, when he had first gone walking with Varlissima in Ithaca, Abrams had written something of conclusive, lifelong significance to him: "In thoroughly absorbed contemplation . . . we . . . share the strength, ease, and grace with which a well-proportioned arch appears to support a bridge."

If this was true—if the sublimation of a feeling could be as beautiful and stable as the arch of a building—then Charles Plumer was right! Everything he hoped to convey to his readers was true. He simply had to build the arch that connected him to others like a trembling web.

Lillian Piasecki and Charles Plumer were already long gone from this world, so he walked with his mother in memory, across a set of ancient wooden bridges in Kyoto. In 1988, two months after Lillian had retired from factory work, mother and son traveled to China, Hong Kong, and Japan. It was the most exotic trip he had taken with his mother in this lifetime.

In 2041, with Colette visiting again, he thought of Abrams once more, and wondered whether his daughter was visiting for the last time. In waking the next morning, he continued to write and live this working text with joy, until his sense of an ending began.

It all made sense now; it had turned out the way it was meant to. His longing and his lived experiences, his hopes and his home, were at equilibrium.

The machinery of his memory had worn down, but the machinery of his family would go on.

AROUND HERE, EVERYONE TALKS LIKE LIONS

Many of the people he came to love had rare skills: to know when to stay and when to go.

He always had the ability to love, even after they had left. In the memories of his old age, he never slept alone.

Everyone came to speak like lions so that he could hear them. They spoke with pride, too, as indirection and nuance were weak second cousins to getting through in the first place.

Walt had said, "All goes onwards and upwards, nothing collapses, and to die is different than what anyone supposed, and luckier." An entire zoo of memories filled his mind now, and it was with pride that he looked across that zoo and called it his own.

He remembered the many times when enemies were near—and someone, somehow, kept them from his door. And for this, he felt thankful.

It was now time for him to surrender graciously. Everyone mattered in his pride. Everyone knew it was time. No one told anyone. Everyone just knew it. He honestly took up his voice and threw her to the wind.

About the Author

Bruce Piasecki is the president and founder of AHC Group, an S advisory Corporation specializing in energy, climate change, and corporate competition. This Group, since 1981, combined in teams the skills of public affairs with strategic communications. For four decades, his set of researchers, strategy advisors, and change management agents had advised over seventy-eight of the Fortune 500, from Merck to Walgreens Boots Alliance, and Suncor Energy.

Dr. Piasecki is the author of twenty books on business strategy, valuation, and corporate change, including the *New York Times* bestseller *Doing More with Less*. That book, now in a paperback remake under *A New Way to Wealth*, became a bestseller in *USA Today, Publisher's Weekly,* and the *Wall Street Journal*. Other editions of Piasecki's books are being remade by his talent agency, www.scottmeredith.com as Rodin Books or other imprints distributed by his first publisher Simon & Schuster. His books are known to align new insights into money, people and rules, especially regarding solutions to climate change and energy innovation, with translations into Japanese, Korean, Greek, Portuguese, Italian and Mandarin.

Upon turning sixty-five, Piasecki reconfigured the board and governance of his organization, making the Group a high-performing, special purpose corporation. Bruce then built an endowed family non-profit arm called The Creative Force Foundation. The Foundation grants Awards from Australia to America to promising writers under forty, contributing solutions to mounting problems on business and society. The Foundation, thanks to its judges and family members, will continue after the death of its founder, by this endowment.

Over time, the themes of this memoir are being uploaded to the crowd-sourced Wikipedia pages. As Walt Whitman suggested, "All goes onwards and upwards . . . and to die is different than what anyone supposed, and luckier."

Other Titles by Bruce Piasecki

Beyond Dumping

America's Future in Hazardous Waste Management

Corporate Environmental Strategy

Corporate Strategy Today

Doing More with Less

Doing More with Teams

Environmental Management and Business Strategy

In Search of Environmental Excellence:
Moving Beyond Blame

New World Companies: The Future of Capitalism

Stray Prayers

The Surprising Solution

World Inc.

2040: A Fable

A New Way to Wealth

The Quiet Genius of Eileen Fisher

Giants of Social Investment

Great Contemporaries:
The Collected Biographies by Bruce Piasecki (pending publication)

Wealth and Climate Competitiveness:
The New Narrative on Business and Society

The Voice of the CEO:
An Anthology on the Path to Climate Competitiveness

Acknowledgments

In a deep emotional sense, each vignette is a form of thanks in this book to the many people who have shaped my sensibility and life. In particular, I wish to thank Frank Weaver, founder of Aplomb Communications, and Arthur Klebanoff, owner of www.scottmeredith. com for their support of my book efforts. And for the loving support provided by my daughter, a doctor, and my wife of nearly half a century, Andrea Carol Masters, I dedicate my work. What follows is nuance.

Most importantly, Ross Tharaud—my lawyer-painter-poet friend—used my completion of this manuscript as an opportunity to tell me how he had risen to my defense back in 1976 during a debate about *Stray Prayers*, my book of poetry. Ross, thanks for allowing me to start.

At my fortieth high school reunion, I read early drafts of these vignettes to fellow classmates—and several wept while reflecting on the recent death of our great teacher Charles Plumer. My 1990 Simon & Schuster editor, André Bernard—a writer himself—gave me help and encouragement during the dog days of my early book assignments, before hitting the bestseller status in 2012.

Writing brings you places—some magical, some taxing, like Istanbul and Tokyo—that you never expected to thrive in. Writing based on travel, business encounters and fear and joy can prove a lonely but majestic path, offering silent glory and a rare chance to make sense of it all. I do not recommend personal narratives to everyone, but it proved illuminating for me.

I have been lucky in most decades of my life, having grown up in the enveloping warmth of my multiracial family with two Puerto Rican foster brothers, an Asian American sister, and a loving, long-living biological sister. We all grew strong from the love of our single mother, Lillian.

Once you read these vignettes, you'll sense the obvious: namely, that my deepest thanks are due to my daughter and wife. I love you both. Forgive this bold trespass into creative writing.